THE OLD FRONT LINE

THE OLD FRONT LINE

by

JOHN MASEFIELD

Preface
by
Martin Middlebrook

with
an introduction on

The Battle of the Somme

by

Col Howard Green, M.C.

PEN & SWORD MILITARY CLASSICS

TO

NEVILLE LYTTON

Originally published in 1917 by William Heinemann,
republished in 1972 by Spurbooks Ltd.
Published in 2003, in this format, by
PEN & SWORD MILITARY CLASSICS
an imprint of
Pen & Sword Books Limited
47, Church Street
Barnsley
S. Yorkshire
S70 2AS

ISBN 0 85052 936 0

A CIP record for this book is
available from the British Library

Printed in England by
CPI UK

CONTENTS

THE BATTLE OF THE SOMME
by
COL HOWARD GREEN, M.C.

THE OLD FRONT LINE
by
JOHN MASEFIELD

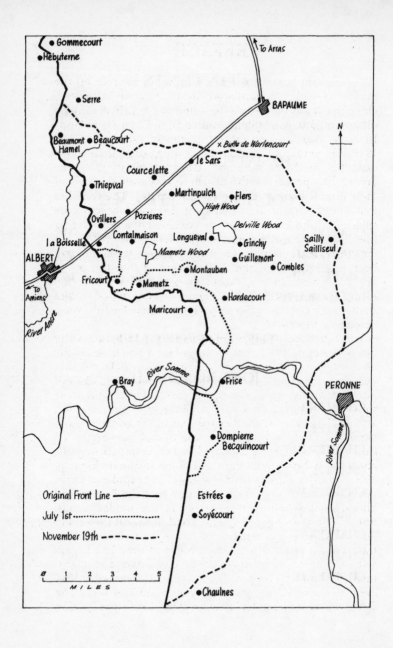

PREFACE

'The old front line' – how that evocative phrase rolls off the tongue so readily by those who visit the Somme battlefield. Of course it was not the *old* front line to the British soldiers of the 4th, 5th, 48th (South Midland) and 51st (Highland) Divisions that came to those trenches in July and August 1915. Desperate to shorten their line after their huge casualties in Champagne and Artois earlier in 1915, the French had persuaded the British to take over this part of their line. It had mostly been a quiet sector. The trenches that would erupt in fierce battle in 1916 and become the subject of John Masefield's book consisted of a meandering line that ran for eighteen miles from the village of Foncquevillers down to the River Somme. It would have been possible to walk the whole length of that line along one continuous trench, except for a few yards where the River Ancre cut through the lines - 'that blood-soaked stream' as a German officer who fought there in 1916 once described it to me.

There had been a live-and-let-live attitude between the two sides before the British came and the French, never the most diligent of trench diggers, handed over defences that were in poor condition. The British commanders did not intend that it should remain a 'cushy' sector and their soldiers were put to work improving the line. But it was still an 'old' front line in another way, consisting of trenches of barely adequate depth, haphazard timber or corrugated iron supports, sagging sandbags, a few cramped dugouts and a flimsy barbed wire barricade. I was fortunate in being able to speak with men from that time. They spoke of heaps of refuse, unearthing stinking corpses that the French had buried in the floor of trenches or in the sandbag walls, hordes of rats and poor hygienic conditions. All they could do was to bring the trenches up to a condition in which a tramp might consent to spend a night or two. The British soldiers had to spend four, six or eight days and nights there over and over again; British generals seemed to like even numbers when organising trench tours of duty. The Germans, by contrast, had been working hard since 1914 to construct impregnable defences in which their men could live in reasonable comfort and safety. There is no need for me to write more on this subject; John Masefield describes the German positions in great detail.

That 'old front line' of Masefield's book was really the two lines of the two enemies separated by a No Man's Land that averaged 350 yards in width, and they were not just the living quarters of soldiers but had an historical perspective. They represented the frontiers of two massive coalitions locked in armed struggle. Private Atkins, on his turn on watch, was the outermost sentinel of the Franco-British alliance determined to push the German invaders back to their fatherland. His opposite number in the German trench performed a similar function for the German and Austro-Hungarian regimes that stretched a thousand miles back to Russia. Here, 'on the Somme', the Germans were equally determined to hold this line 70 miles deep into France to which they had advanced in 1914.

By the end of June 1916 the British and French were ready to mount the great offensive that they hoped would bring them victory. As is well known, that great effort commenced at 7.30 am on the first day of July; the outcome is also well known and need not be dwelled upon here. By the autumn, over a million British soldiers had either attacked from the old front line or had passed over it for later actions, many making the trip two or three times; all had been aware of its significance. 'We moved up, crossing the old front line', the survivors would later write in their accounts. But more than 100,000 of those British soldiers never made the return journey. At the point of greatest advance, the line had only moved seven miles. In some places - in front of Gommecourt and Serre - the German defence was so strong that not a yard of ground was gained; the old front line remained the old front line until the Germans voluntarily gave up the ground in 1917.

John Masefield had gone out to Gallipoli during the campaign there in 1915 and had immediately published a small book describing the terrain and the conditions under which the United Kingdom and Anzac troops had to fight. For this next book, he obviously visited the Somme before the battle was finished. The single map in the book shows the old British line only from Thiepval Wood to Montauban and only the positions reached by the advance on 27 July, a date of no particular significance. The villages of Thiepval, Courcelette, Martinpuich, Flers, Ginchy and Guillemont are shown as still being in German hands. But he did not intend his book to cover the whole battle; he only wanted to describe the original line from which the offensive was launched. It was really the first battlefield guide of the Somme. On page 31 he writes:

> It may be some years before those whose fathers, husbands and brothers were killed in this great battle, may be able to visit the battlefield where their dead are buried. Perhaps many of them, from brooding on the map, and from dreams and visions in the night, have in their minds an image or picture of that place. The following pages may help some few others, who have not already formed that image, to see the scene as it appears to-day. What it was like on the day of battle cannot be imagined by those who were not there.

He concludes his book with the scene at zero hour on the first day in these words:

> The men of the first wave climbed up the parapets, in tumult, darkness, and the presence of death, and having done with all pleasant things, advanced across the No Man's Land to begin the Battle of the Somme.

Masefield was a poet and wrote in such lyrical terms. At the time that he sent his manuscript to his publisher, he did not know of the disappointment and exhausting stagnation in front of the Butte of Warlencourt and on the Transloy Ridge at the end of the battle in November.

John Masefield may have expected the relatives of the soldiers of the Somme to visit the battlefield after the war but he would have been surprised, I think, if he had known of the intense interest that would bring so many to walk his 'old front line' nearly a century later. I am pleased his book is being reprinted. I had a copy once but somehow became parted from it. Now it is back, like an old friend.

Martin Middlebrook, author of *The First Day on the Somme*.

HIGH WOOD

Ladies and gentlemen, this is High Wood
Called by the French, Bois des Fourneaux,
The famous spot which in Nineteen-Sixteen,
July, August and September was the scene
Of long and bitterly contested strife,
By reason of its High commanding site.
Observe the effect of shell-fire in the trees
Standing and fallen ; here is wire ; this trench
For months inhabited, twelve times changed hands ;
(They soon fall in), used later as a grave.
It has been said on good authority
That in the fighting for this patch of wood
Were killed somewhere above eight thousand men,
Of whom the greater part were buried here,
This mound on which you stand being . . .
                                        Madame, please,
You are requested kindly not to touch
Or take away the Company's property
As souvenirs ; you'll find we have on sale
A large variety, all guaranteed.
As I was saying, all is as it was,
This is an unknown British officer,
The tunic having lately rotted off.
Please follow me – this way . . .
                                the *path*, sir, *please*,
The ground which was secured at great expense
The Company keeps absolutely untouched
And in that dug-out (genuine) we provide
Refreshments at a reasonable rate.
You are requested not to leave about
Paper, or ginger-beer bottles, or orange-peel,
There are waste-paper baskets at the gate.
                                Philip Johnstone
                                        1918

THE BATTLE OF THE SOMME

CHAPTER I

THE series of actions known to history as The Battle of the Somme consisted in fact of twelve battles. These were the battles of Albert, Bazentin Ridge, Delville Wood, Pozières Ridge, Guillemont, Ginchy, Flers-Courcelette, Morval, Thiepval Ridge, Transloy Ridge, Ancre Heights, and Ancre 1916.

The battle was the most terrible in British history. It killed or maimed over one million, two hundred thousand men, over half a million of them British. It has been said, with truth, that the flower of the British Empire died on the Somme. It broke the back of the German field army, and killed the cream of their infantry, then the finest professional troops in Europe. For the men who fought there, and the nations they fought for, it was never the same after the Somme. The songs, the writing, the poetry, became cynical, after the Somme.

The battle lasted, officially, from July 1, 1916, until November 18. It had been planned and prepared for months before the infantry assault on July 1, and the fighting went on steadily after November, until the Germans eventually withdrew to the Hindenburg Line in the spring of the following year.

In simple terms, the object of the battle, as in all preceding and subsequent battles on the Western Front, was to break through the enemy defence system, bring up the cavalry, and end the stalemate that had prevailed in France since the trench line raced across Europe in the Autumn of 1914. The basic cause of this stalemate was that the war weapons of the period were in check. The weapons of defence commanded the battlefield, the shrapnel shell, the machine-gun, and barbed wire. Men, unprotected, could not go against these weapons with any hope of success, while at the same time the prospect of ending the war without fighting was remote. The Germans held Belgium, Luxemburg, much of Northern France and had made significant territorial gains elsewhere. Their armies were excellently trained, and well equipped. They had developed their early positions and shell scrapes into an extremely formidable defence system behind which they intended to stay, defying eviction.

The war went on with successes to either side, on other fronts, in Mesopotamia, East Africa, Salonika, Russia, the Balkans, and at sea. But it became clear very early on that the prime theatre of operations would be Western Europe and that the war would be won or lost on the Western Front. By 1916 the Western Front had begun to fascinate and horrify the men who fought there. The Front added words to the nation's speech. Men who died in France had "gone west," or were "on the wire." Both sides still believed that somehow a breakthrough could come, and the stalemate be ended, although the battles in 1914 and 1915 had produced long casualty lists, and very little else. During the autumn of 1915 both sides planned, trained, and waited for the further conflicts that the New Year would certainly bring. On the Allied side, they waited especially for the arrival of the New Armies, the "Kitchener" armies raised by the great Field Marshal and the "Big Push" that their presence could make possible.

The British nation that went to war in 1914, was not a major military power in Europe. The Army, whilst highly skilled in field craft and weapon training, was small, designed mainly to fight colonial wars on far-off frontiers. There was, of course, a Territorial Army, but this was trained and equipped for home service, and Britain's power rested mainly on her strong economy, and the Royal Navy. When war broke out, the original B.E.F. that went to France, consisted of two infantry corps, each of two divisions, and a cavalry division. Later they were joined by other elements of the Regular Army who came home from garrisons all over the world to fight in France. It was a wonderful army, a professional force; the finest army the British people have ever had. But it was small.

In 1914, the French, the Germans and the Austro-Hungarians numbered their armies in millions. They had men, trained and equipped to man massive field armies, both currently serving and on reserve. They also had conscription. It was not until 1916, almost two years after the outbreak of war that the British introduced compulsory service. When Lord Kitchener in August 1914, issued his famous call, backed with his ''Your King and Country Need You'' poster, he had realized that this war, in spite of popular hopes, would not be over by Christmas, as was confidently believed, and that large armies on the continental pattern would be needed. He did not, however, realize the effect his call would have. He wanted, at first, a hundred thousand men. Over a million volunteers had flocked to the Colours by February 1915.

The Army staggered. There were no facilities, no depots, uniforms, weapons, boots, or equipment for such numbers. Worse, there were no instructors. Nearly every able N.C.O. was in France. But there was no holding back the will of the volunteers. They raised companies and battalions themselves in the cities and small towns. Regiments often had battalions of men from a particular town or industrial firm who joined up, determined to train, soldier, and then fight together in France. This fact, as much as any other, contributed to the tragedy of the Somme Battle. When a battalion "went over the top" and met the machine-guns a whole town might go into mourning. The long lists of similar names on war memorials is due to that first great outburst of enthusiasm. And yet, there were advantages. The men knew each other, were friends, and understood each other's ways. In that initial volunteering, whole stratas of a society, much more rigid and class conscious than that of to-day met, and grew to respect and admire each other. The middle classes provided the officers, but they lived and worked with men, working men, whom they would never have met outside the ranks of the Army.

Charles Carrington, later a subaltern on the Somme, remembers his time in training. "It was not the comfort of being a man on a salary, nor the fun in the officers' mess, nor the pony riding, but another factor that made my year so satisfying. I was in love with my platoon. The whole of my affection and thoughts were for forty Yorkshire miners with whom my life was so unexpectedly linked . . . the 9th Yorks and Lancasters were colliers from the West Riding, a rough tough lot, and if there are better or braver men in the

world I have yet to find them.'' His diary noted—
''I shall never think of the lower classes again in the
same way after the War.''

So something was gained, and added, never really to
be lost ; comradeship. A sense of togetherness, that
only those who were in it together could feel, remember,
or be entitled to share. This brotherliness is in evidence
to-day with the original 1914 Kitchener battalion's
re-unions, which once a year still gather their men
together, none of them under seventy.

The German Army, in early 1916, was the finest in
Europe. The losses of earlier campaigns had been made
up, largely from reserves. The Germans had improved
their defences during the winter, and planned to make
1916 the year of decision. Not that they planned an
offensive as practised by the Allies. The Germans had
seen enough of the enemy withering in front of their
wire not to realize how assaults against machine-guns
could end. The Germans had other plans. They
planned to threaten the French bastion of Verdun, and
attack a position which, for various reasons, the
French could never abandon. To retain that city
the French must commit every man they had, and the
German artillery would pound them to powder on the
''anvil'' of Verdun. The German objective for 1916
was to bleed the French Army to death. While the

French, as 1915 drew to a close, waited for fine weather, for the new English Armies to pull their weight and take on a greater share of the burden, and whilst waiting, they planned.

It was, therefore, during a period of comparative inactivity that General Sir Douglas Haig took command of the British Expeditionary Force in December 1915. The instructions given to Sir Douglas Haig on taking up his appointment directed him, ''To avoid heavy losses and wastage, to co-operate most sympathetically with the plans and wishes of our Ally (the French),'' yet whilst the closest co-operation between the French and British as a united army must be the governing policy, his was an independent command. In short to go along with the French on every possible occasion, short of commitment to outright disaster. These were difficult instructions, reflecting a difficult situation, and stemming from the fact that there was no Supreme Commander for the Allied Armies in France. Co-operation, not command, was the rule, and much of the wasted effort, disunity, lack of success, and loss of life on the Western Front was a direct result of this lack of overall direction.

In an attempt to achieve greater unity of effort, General Joffre, the French Commander-in-Chief had, in 1915, begun a series of Inter-Allied Conferences, held in his headquarters at Chantilly. At one of these, early in 1916, the French proposed the idea of a general offensive on the Western Front, with the French under Foch attacking with forty divisions south of the Somme, and the British, with say, twenty-five divisions of their New Armies joining the attack north of the river. The French maintained that the possibility of success would be great. Haig demurred. He had plans of his own for an attack further north, around Messines. However, he had his instructions to co-operate with the French, and since they seemed determined to stage an offensive on the Somme, where the French and British sectors met, it seemed he would have to support them. This, in essence, summed up relations at higher command through the greater part of the war. The British maintained Allied unity, by giving in to French wishes. The French achieved their ends by a combination of pressure and petulance with which later generations are not unfamiliar. The only real reason for the French wishing to attack on the Somme, was that here, at the junction of the Allied line, the English were bound to take part.

General Joffre, in pressing his plan on Haig, stressed that the area north of the Somme was a quiet sector, and that the ground favoured an assault. The first point begged a further question, and the second was untrue. The sector, previously French, was quiet, but this quietness had been used by the Germans to fortify a position already naturally strong, and make it virtually impregnable. In fact the German positions north of the Somme were a series of fortresses where, in addition, the ground permitted almost total observation of the proposed British assault areas. In spite of considering alternative plans, by February, the Allies were committed to a joint offensive on the Somme, when on February 21, the Germans unleashed their assault on the city and fortress of Verdun.

When it became apparent, on February 22, that the Verdun attack was serious, General Joffre asked that the British should relieve sixteen French divisions in the line, to allow their transfer to Verdun. Haig agreed to this, and the replacement of French divisions by those of the British began. It must be remembered that even at its fullest extent the British sector of the Front was no more than seventy miles, a bare 25 per cent of the total line. Apart from six Belgium divisions in the north, the rest was held by the French, who felt, not unreasonably, that the British, with their immense resources, could have taken over more of the burden. However, if the English line was shorter than the French, it was far more active. The French, unless an offensive was actually in progress, had a sensible ''live and let live'' policy with the Germans opposite. Not so the British. When the British took over a sector of the line, they would tidy up the trenches, spend a few days improving the wire and dugouts, and then, after a few shells to advise the Germans that the palmy days were over, they would go all out to gain the upper hand. Regular shellings and machine-gunning of the German line, mining, fighting patrols to dominate No Man's Land, and trench raids all started. While showing the right offensive spirit, this policy was not entirely wise. The Germans generally held the advantage of ground, they had the heavier guns, and were no mean trench fighters themselves. On balance the British policy probably cost more lives than it gained advantages. Nevertheless, as the German assault gained momentum at Verdun, and more French divisions were pulled out of the line elsewhere to meet it, the French contribution to the Somme offensive gradually shrank.

On March 1, 1916, General Sir Henry Rawlinson took command of the newly formed 4th Army which began to occupy the line, north of the Somme, between Hebuterne and Maricourt, a distance of some seventeen miles. The right flank of the 4th Army joined the left or northern flank of the French 6th Army. The German positions opposite the Allies were manned by the German 2nd Army. General Rawlinson was directed to plan an offensive, in co-operation with the French with ''Z Day,'' the day of the infantry assault, on or about July 1. General Rawlinson was a careful man,

a professional soldier, and of great experience. With
these instructions in mind he began his preparations
with a careful personal study of the ground. He can
hardly have liked what he saw.

The country north of the Somme is very like Wiltshire. The Somme and its northern tributary, the
Ancre, cut deep valleys through the land, which runs
in high irregular spurs down to the lower ground.
Woods dot the hills and valleys, and on the spurs or
sheltering in the re-entrants between them are a
number of small villages. A road runs across the
battlefield, straight as an arrow up the axis of the
proposed attack, from the town of Albert, through
La Boiselle, Pozières and Le Sars to Baupaume. It is
an old Roman road and the villages along it and to
either side, Thiepval, Longeval, Flers, Courcelette,
Le Sars, would prove to be fortresses in the German line.
From the southern end the German line cut across the
Somme near Curlu, then behind Maricourt round the
front of Fricourt and Mametz, across the road through
La Boisselle, Ovillers, in front of Thiepval, and then
across the Ancre below Beaumont Hamel to cross the
gently rolling plateau to Gommecourt, which lay just
inside the German line, facing the British in Hebuterne
and Fonquevilliers. About a mile behind the front line
lay another line which took in such places as Delville
Wood, Guillemont, Flers and Grandcourt. There was

a third undug line behind that, in front of Baupaume.
The spurs, especially in the area of Thiepval, north of
the Albert-Baupaume road, and around Fricourt and
Mametz to the south, favoured the Germans, giving
them observation over the British line, and enabling
the German strongpoints in every wood and village, to
support each other with enfilade rifle and machine-gun
fire. It was a formidable position, and General
Rawlinson laid careful plans for his assault upon it.

His laudable intention was to provide his men with
a walkover. Given local air superiority, he would
range his artillery on the German wire and trenches
and pound them to bits in the week before ''Z Day.''
The trenches would be levelled and untenable, the wire
cut and scattered. Difficult salients would be mined
and blown sky high at Zero hour. The advance of the
assault battalions would be co-ordinated with the final
artillery bombardment, and the infantry would walk
behind the artillery barrage up to and over the German
positions. For this reason he laid down rigid instructions for the assaulting battalions, giving them a
controlled rate of advance of so many yards per minute.
This pace was deliberately slow, and designed to keep
up with the pre-arranged advance of the shellfire. No
rushes were to be permitted, no infiltration. There
would after all be no need to rush, as the enemy would
be pulverized and unable to resist.

As we shall see, this plan went wrong. The Somme country is clay on top of chalk. This absorbs the effect of shellfire and in their deep dugouts, the Germans, while suffering hunger, thirst and having casualties which they could not evacuate, nevertheless survived. Moreover, Rawlinson did not have heavy guns powerful enough to shatter the deep dugouts, while observation in many places favoured the Germans. Belts of wire remained uncut, and in other places the Germans emerged at night to repair the damage of the day's barrage. Constant shelling churned up the ground which would later help to slow the assault waves down. Finally, the Germans had many guns which outranged those of the British, and which even if discovered from the air, could not be hit. Others deliberately remained silent, unsuspected, waiting to fire on " Z Day."

General Rawlinson's Fourth Army consisted of eighteen infantry divisions, each of about twenty thousand men, divided into six Corps. Eleven of these divisions would assault on ''Z Day.'' On his left flank he had the assistance of two divisions of Allenby's 3rd Army, the 46th Division and the 56th Division, to assault the German strongpoint salient of Gommecourt. A Reserve Army under General Gough, later the 5th Army, was mustering south of Albert. Seven of the 4th Army Divisions were Kitchener's Army Divisions.

They were unseasoned troops and many would be going into action for the first time.

While Rawlinson and his men prepared for their part in the great Anglo-French offensive, the situation on the French side was deteriorating. During March, April and May the Germans pounded and assaulted the positions around Verdun. The battle there became a mincing machine, chopping up divisions as they were fed into the line. The assault on the Somme was becoming increasingly necessary in order to relieve the pressure on Verdun, while at the same time the French were wondering how they could continue to fight at Verdun, and yet play a part on the Somme. Inevitably, something had to give. The original forty division attack had shrunk in area and manpower as the French contribution to the forthcoming push was necessarily reduced, finally to sixteen divisions, of which five actually attacked on an eight mile front on July 1.

Meanwhile, French pressure on the British to open the Somme offensive mounted. Haig was adamant. He needed time to prepare and would not assault until he was ready, which would be on or about July 1. He finally fixed June 28 as "Z Day." At the last the French wanted a small delay and the assault was put back until 7.30 a.m. on Saturday, July 1.

On the German side the offensive was awaited with quiet confidence. The only question was when it would come. As the battle of Verdun went on the German Command knew that a relief offensive must follow from the Allied side, and supposed that the British New Armies would simply advance the date of their attack. Information trickled in, all confirming the build-up across the line. They could see the observation balloons of the British Division, interrogate prisoners, and hear the rumble of vehicles bringing men and munitions to the front. Much information came from British newspapers obtained in neutral countries. On June 2, for example, the British Minister of Labour gave a clue in a speech to munition workers. He said, ''I am asked why the Whitsuntide holidays are to be postponed until the end of July. How inquisitive we all are ! ! It should suffice that we ask for postponement of the holidays, and to the end of July. This fact should speak volumes.'' The German Crown Prince Rupprecht commented, ''It does so speak. It is the clearest indication that there will be a great British offensive in a few weeks.'' The Germans knew the attack was coming, but they were not sure where ; for seen from the German observation points above the Ancre, the British preparations seemed so blatant to constitute a deliberate deception.

By the middle of June, the final preparations were in hand. Immense amounts of work had been done, from tactical training, down to a vast support programme, with new roads, railways, water-lines, dumps and, ominously, dressing and casualty clearing stations springing up everywhere. Hundreds of guns had come up, and now, ranged on their targets, they waited to commence the introductory barrage. Finally, as the month neared its end, the assault battalions marched up to positions near the line.

Henry Williamson remembers. ''They marched through villages of line-washed pisè and thatch, where children stood and stared, but waved no more ; for hundreds of thousands of Les Anglais had already passed that way, singing, whistling and shouting the same remarks.''

If relations between the British and French commands were sometimes tense, those between the troops and the French civilians remained fairly good. The original enthusiasm of 1914 had, of course, waned and the French peasants or shop-keepers in the towns behind the lines now regarded the British soldiers as something apart, not super-men, but quite pleasant. They adopted an almost paternal attitude to them and never forgot that the men out of the trenches had money to spend. The troops in turn believed, incorrectly, that the British Army paid the French Government rent for their trenches, and worse, and correctly, that the French watered down their beer.

At six a.m. on June 24, with a force and noise that carried across the downlands and sea to the outskirts of London, the artillery barrage began. One thousand five hundred and thirty-seven guns, one to every twenty yards of front began pounding the German trenches. Only four hundred and sixty-seven of these guns were heavy. But it looked good, and it went on for days, the German line disappearing in a churned-up cloud of dust and chalk. Surely nothing could live after that. To prevent the wire being repaired by night, trench raids were carried out on the German line. Not many were successful. On the 8th Corp front, no entry was made into the German position, and the enemy trenches seemed to be full of men. Reports on wire cutting varied from ''very much damaged,'' to ''not properly cut.'' Battalions reporting this unplesaant fact to their divisions were told they were ''windy.'' So the barrage went on, day after day. No supplies could reach the German trenches. They would be getting hungry, tired, shocked by the blasting, unable to evacuate their wounded, perhaps unable to resist.

On the night of June 30, the assault battalions moved up into the line. Each man carried a minimum of 66 lbs of kit, over half a hundredweight of equipment to carry across the shell-torn No Man's Land, and fight with on the other side. Under such a burden the most that could be managed was a steady walk. Many men carried even great loads, spare Lewis guns, ammunition, water and supplies.   But since it was going to be a walkover, no haste would be necessary.

Dawn came, misty in the valleys, promising a hot day. It got light around 4 a.m., and the final artillery barrage began, improving in volume and accuracy as the mist cleared.   As the minutes ticked to Zero, this barrage rose in intensity, the enemy line dancing under the continuous explosions.   Then, at 7.30 precisely, the barrage lifted, and on a seventeen-mile front, one hundred and ten thousand British infantrymen went over the top.

CHAPTER II

July 1st

Let us see what the Germans saw at 7.30 a.m. on July 1 :

"At 7.30 a.m. the hurricane of shells ceased as suddenly as it had begun. Our men at once clambered up the steep shafts leading from the dug-outs to daylight and ran for the nearest shell craters. The machine-guns were pulled out of the dug-outs and hurriedly placed into position, their crews dragging the heavy ammunition boxes up the steps and out to the guns. A rough firing line was thus rapidly established. As soon as in position, a series of extended lines of British infantry were seen moving forward from the British trenches. The first line appeared to continue without end to right and left. It was quickly followed by a second line, then a third and fourth. They came on at a steady easy pace as if expecting to find nothing alive in our front trenches. . . . The front line, preceded by a thin line of skirmishers and bombers, was now half-way across No Man's Land. 'Get ready,' was passed along our front from crater to crater, and heads appeared over the crater edges as final positions were taken up for the best view and machine-guns mounted firmly in place. A few minutes later, when the leading British line was within 100 yards, the rattle of machine-guns and rifle fire broke out from along the whole line of craters. Some fired kneeling so as to get a better target over the broken ground, while others in the excitement of the moment stood up, regardless of their own safety, to fire into the crowd of men in front of them. The advance rapidly crumpled under this hail of shells and bullets. All along the line men could be seen throwing their arms into the air and collapsing never to move again. Badly wounded rolled about in their agony, and others less severely injured crawled to the nearest shell-hole. The noise of battle became indescribable. The shouting of orders and the shrill British cheers as they charged forward could be heard above the violent and intense fusilade of machine-guns and the bursting bombs, and above the deep thundering of the artillery and the shell explosions. With all this were mingled the moans and groans of the wounded, the cries for help and the last screams of death. Again and again the extended lines of British infantry broke against the German defence like waves against a cliff, only to be beaten back. It was an amazing spectacle of un-exampled gallantry, courage and bull-dog determination on both sides.''

It was the same all along the front. The fact now being painfully grasped was that artillery alone could not snuff out every machine-gun post, and yet just one machine-gun could rip a battalion to pieces. And there were scores of them in action, firing from concrete dugouts or the lips of the shell craters. Never again would they have such a target. The width of No Man's Land contributed to the casualties allowing two or three lines of infantry to get into the open, ready to be mown down as, stumbling across the ground, weighted down with their equipment and sticking to the time schedule behind the barrage, they pressed on.

In the north, at Gommecourt, two divisions of Allenby's 3rd Army attacked the German defences in Gommecourt Village and Park. This was a subsidiary offensive, designed to shorten the front of the 4th Army, and divert enemy attention from the attacks to the south. The VII Corps had been deliberately open in their preparations, and knew that the Germans were expecting them.

Gommecourt was a strong position, a salient projecting into the British line and they attacked it from both sides ; from the north, the 46th Division, men from Staffordshire, Lincoln and Leicester, and from the south the 56th Division of London Territorials.

The 46th advanced at zero hour in six waves, and under cover of smoke. Unfortunately the smoke was so thick that platoons got lost in it, and the advance was disrupted. The wire in front of the German position was found still uncut, and as this horrifying fact was discovered, down came the German artillery barrage, and machine-gunners up from the deep dug-outs, opened fire.

All the assault battalions were strongly resisted by machine-guns, rifle fire and artillery, but the attacks went on, alternating with barrage and counter barrage, throughout the day. By nightfall, the casualties in some battalions had reached 80 per cent, and the attack had been completely repulsed. The 46th Division had been supposed to link up behind the objective with the 56th (London) Division attacking the salient from the south. When the Germans realized, and it didn't take them very long, that they were in little danger on the northern flank, they turned the whole of their attention on the Londoners.

The 56th had left their trenches before zero hour, under cover of smoke, and lay out in No Man's Land waiting for the barrage to lift. The German wire was well cut, and as the shelling lifted, the Londoners were

in the German front-line trench before the enemy had
time to oppose them. They also overran the second
trench, but had a hard struggle to overcome and capture
the third. In doing so they used up most of their
ammunition, and the enemy counter barrage now
falling on No Man's Land, prevented support from
coming up, bringing water, ammunition and most
important, more grenades. The battalions lodged in
the German trenches were cut off, and the Germans
massed to expel them. Heavy shelling was followed by
infantry attacks. The Londoners held out as long as
their ammunition and grenades lasted, but an attempt
to re-inforce them in the early afternoon led to two
companies of the 2nd London Regiment (Royal
Fusiliers) being annihilated by machine-gun fire while
crossing No Man's Land. At dusk, having fought alone,
all day the elements came back. Over 1,300 men
never came back at all, but lay dead in No Man's Land
or the enemy position. The London Scottish lost
fourteen officers and six hundred and two men, all
of whom were officer material, out of twenty-four
officers and eight hundred and forty-seven men
engaged. No Man's Land was carpeted with the
wounded and as it grew light on July 2, firing ceased
as the dead and wounded were brought in.

Almost everywhere along the Front, the German Army
ceased fire whenever possible after the attack subsided,

and assisted in the evacuation of the British wounded. This was a decent and chivalrous act, and it should be remembered.

South of the VII Corp, in Allenby's Army, lay the VIII Corp in General Rawlinson's. The VIII Corp, commanded by Lt.-Gen. Hunter-Weston, was charged with the capture of Beaumont Hamel, a small village lying between two spurs which ran down to the Ancre. The northern spur was known as Redan Ridge and the southern as Hawthorn Ridge. The German line crossed these spurs, and ran off north by the village of Serre, which was to menace the left flank of VIII Corp as they attacked Beaumont Hamel. As usual the Germans had a formidable position, with trenched redoubts on the ridges around Beaumont Hamel as strongpoints above the village itself. There was also, in the south side of Hawthorn Ridge a shallow valley running up towards the British line, in which lay a deep cutting. This was known as the " Y " Ravine and is a freak of nature. About thirty feet deep, forty yards wide, and with very steeply sloping banks, it made perfect cover from all except extremely plunging fire from field howitzers. Consequently, although only a few yards behind the enemy's front-line trench, it was filled with company battalion headquarters, First-Aid posts, ammunition stores, cook-houses, etc., while into the lip of the west-facing bank were built machine-gun

ran into the concentrated fire of three machine-guns
and lost three hundred and seventy-two men in the
first five minutes. The British assault trenches were
now being shelled and many men in the forward
battalions never got clear, but were hit and lay clogging
up the trenches, impeding the arrival of fresh troops
and their own evacuation. The wire was reasonably
cut, but naturally men bunched to get through the
gaps, and made a perfect target for the machine-guns.
The dead lay in heaps at the gaps.

At nine o'clock, believing for some reason that only
a few isolated machine-guns were still delaying the
advance, the Divisional Commander sent two of his
reserve battalions—the 1st Essex and the Newfoundland Regiment—to attack the western end of the " Y "
Ravine. Such was the congestion and confusion
wrought by shelling in the British trenches that the
Essex was held up and arrived late, while the Newfoundland Regiment, reaching the open, attacked
alone.

Newfoundland was a sparsely populated part of the
Empire, which had nevertheless raised a regiment of
one battalion to fight in Europe. They had already
served at Gallipoli, and this was their first fight in
France. No sooner had the advance began than
machine-guns hidden in the "Y" Ravine began to rake
their ranks. With superb courage the Newfound-

landers pressed home their attack across No Man's Land, dropping men at every step. Only a handful reached the German position, where they were quickly shot down. It is not often in modern war that a regiment is annihilated, but this one was. The New-foundlanders had seven hundred and ten casualties, including all the officers, and the regiment ceased for a while to exist. The Essex, coming up later also suffered severely when they advanced on the German line. By 10.30, news of this and other disasters had reached the Divisional H.Q., and all attacks were stopped. The barrage which, according to plan had gone on across the objective, was brought back to pound the enemy trenches again.

VIII Corp continued attacking throughout the day, achieving nothing. There had been no surprise, the enemy machine-guns were in action everywhere, his barrage was devastating and his deep dugouts full of infantry, ready to repel the assault and kill what few men penetrated the trenches.

It took three days to clear the wounded from No Man's Land in front of VIII Corp. Here again the Germans allowed an informal truce, and helped with the casualties. VIII Corp suffered the heaviest casualties of the day, over fourteen thousand men, killed, wounded and missing, and nothing was gained. Beaumont Hamel held out almost to the end of the

Battle, finally falling on November 14, only four days before the offensive was finally stopped, in mud and snow showers ; an offensive that had started not a mile away four months before, in the high heat of summer.

Across the Ancre, the X Corp had, as its main task, the reduction of Thiepval. Thiepval was one of the great bastions in the German line. The Thiepval plateau stands on a pronounced hill above the Ancre, over-looking the village of Hamel, and Aveluy Wood, both in British hands. Thiepval village, a small place of about sixty buildings, had been turned into a fortress, like all the villages immediately behind the front line, with concrete reinforced cellars containing machine-gun nests, and stocked with food, water and ammunition. Belts of wire and deep communication trenches ran off everywhere. Thiepval was further protected on either flank by two huge networks of enclosed trenches, known as the Schwaben and Leipzig Redoubts.

Apart from the strength of Thiepval itself the defences were in great depth, stretching back two miles to connect with Mouquet Farm in the rear, and the trenches to the south around Ovillers. The Germans garrisoning this fortress were full of fight and had replied vigorously to British shell-fire. Previous attempts at raiding their trenches had been repulsed, and it was clear that the continuous bombardment of the past seven days had done little damage to the deep dugouts. However battalion commanders who reported back to their Divisional H.Q.'s that the German machine-guns were undamaged were curtly told that they were scared.

The X Corp's task was to capture the complete spur in their first onslaught on July 1. Just before bombardment reached its crescendo, gas was released and drifted slowly towards the German lines. But to no avail. When the troops went over the top they met a hail of fire.

The 36th (Ulster) Division spearheaded the attack against the centre of the Thiepval position. This was a New Army formation, and on that day in their first big battle they had a special enthusiasm for the attack, for July 1 is the true anniversary of the Battle of the Boyne, now celebrated on July 12. Most of the men had been in Carson's Ulster Volunteers resisting Home Rule in 1914, and were full of a fervent and religious dedication.

At 7.30, bugles blew along the line and the Ulstermen rose from their trenches and advanced up the hill. The wire was well cut and they swept over the German position with few casualties. By 8.30 they had advanced nearly a mile and were in possession of most of the 1st and 2nd line German defences. Except on the left, where machine-guns in the village of St. Pierre Divan had savaged them, all was going well. Just across the Ancre however, the Irish regiments attacking Beaucourt station were mowed down.

The other assault division of X Corp, the 32nd, had meanwhile overrun the Leipzig Redoubt and the battle, with a few checks, seemed to be going as planned. Tragedy however, lay waiting. Advancing faster than expected, so swift had been their success, three battalions ran into the supporting British barrage and suffered heavy casualties from their own guns. This check gave the Germans in the rear of the Thiepval position time to organize and counter-attack.

By mid morning the position was becoming clear. The 36th Division had thrust itself between Thiepval and St. Pierre Divion, and held most of the Thiepval spur. They also held, just, Stuff Redoubt in the rear of the German position on the plateau. But Thiepval itself still held out, indeed the fire from there mounted steadily and enfiladed all advance, especially that of the supporting battalions. Shelling had also increased and No Man's Land became virtually impassible. Slowly, as the day wore on, the Irish hold on the Thiepval spur began to slip. Ammunition ran out, and German infantry began to bomb their way along the communication trenches into the Schwaben position while more Germans emerged from deep dugouts and took the Ulstermen in the rear.

At 10 p.m. that night, having held the position all

day and ammunition almost exhausted, they faced a major counter-attack from three sides. It was the last straw and the 36th Division withdrew. They had penetrated almost a mile into the main German position to the north of Thiepval but in doing so they had lost over five thousand men. The 32nd Division, less exposed, clung grimly to their toe-hold in the Liepzig Salient. They could do no more. X Corp lost over nine thousand men in all, and it was later said that only bullet proof soldiers could have taken Thiepval that day. Thiepval finally fell on September 26, eleven weeks after the first assault.

In the centre of the 4th Army was III Corp, astride the road from Albert to Baupaume which ran up the axis of the intended advance. The objective of III Corp was Pozières, which stood on a low ridge about two miles behind the German line. No Man's Land in front of III Corp was narrower than usual, and at one point known as the "Glory Hole," opposite La Boisselle, it narrowed to less than fifty yards.

The main strength of the German position lay in two fortified villages, La Boisselle which lay on the Albert-Baupaume road directly in the German front line, and Ovillers which, viewed from the Old Front Line, lay to the left of La Boisselle, across a shallow re-entrant known as Mash Valley. To the right of La Boisselle lay another re-entrant reaching up to Contalmaison, known as Sausage Valley. La Boisselle and Ovillers, like so many other villages, lay on spurs, which gave them visibility over the British line and made their defences mutually supporting. III Corp had two assault divisions, the 8th, an old regular Army division now with many New Army soldiers in its ranks, and the 34th, a New Army formation raised mainly in the north of England. The infantry commanders were far from satisfied with the effect that the artillery fire had had on the German front.

Because the German line curved back from La Boisselle, placing the proposed assault areas up Mash and Sausage Valleys in enfilade, two great mines were dug under the German line at La Boisselle and prepared for detonation at zero hour. It was estimated that, apart from destroying the machine positions, these explosions would throw up sufficient chalk to mask the advancing troops from the fire of the flanking machine-guns. At zero hour, 34th Division sent twelve battalions against La Boisselle behind a lifting barrage. By 7.40, ten minutes after going over the top, 80 per cent of these men were casualties, of whom two thousand seven hundred were killed. Heavy machine-gun fire decimated the ranks, and although the mines at " Y-sap," beside La Boisselle and at " Lochnager," by Sausage Valley, went up successfully, the Germans were quick to occupy the craters and machine-gun the advancing infantry. The right brigade of the 34th Division, however, met with considerable success, and two battalions penetrated the enemy lines and held the southern edges of La Boisselle. They were the first troops in the 4th Army to make and retain a lodgement in the enemy defences.

The 8th Division attacked Ovillers, advancing up Mash Valley and Nab Valley on the far side of the Ovillers spur. Only isolated detachments got as far as the German line. Crossfire from Ovillers and La Boisselle, and long-range fire from Thiepval knocked the battalions to pieces. Ovillers and most of La Boisselle remained uncaptured, and III Corp held only a small gain on the right flank near Sausage Valley to show in return for their losses. Here again, although the night of July 1 was comparatively quiet, the problem of casualty evacuation remained. It took until July 3 to remove all the wounded from the battlefield.

It is not easy, among all the individual scenes that are worth recounting on every sector of the front, to give a simple guideline to events. Overall it is fair to say that the British advance enjoyed far more success as the line moved south. North of the Albert-Baupaume road all was disaster. South of it the situation gradually improved, with the small gain on the right flank of the III Corp as the first slender sign

of changing fortune. Success, in these terms, is a
relative phrase. Casualties were appalling, and as we
shall see the successes on the right were not exploited
as they should have been, and the foundations were
thereby laid for much grief in the future. But for the
moment, something at last was being achieved.

To the right of III Corp now being hammered at
La Boisselle, lay XV Corp, charged with overrunning
the defences of Fricourt and Mametz. The German
line here, as elsewhere, was strong. The villages were
fortresses, the dugouts deep and comfortable and even
provided in some cases with electricity ; the trench
system was intricate and well wired.

However, the preliminary bombardment here had
succeeded in locating and almost silencing the German
artillery. The defence relied mainly on machine-guns.
The main positions around Fricourt and Mametz were
not to be attacked directly, but rather surrounded,
and it was arranged to screen the advancing troops with
smoke laid down by mortar fire. The British Army
at this time made very little use of smoke. There
seems no real real reason for this as the smoke bomb
was available and the means to discharge it well known.
It seems that the use of smoke had not yet caught on,
and was therefore rarely written into operational
plans.

The 21st Division was to surround and capture

Fricourt, and at the start all went well. No Man's Land was narrow at this point and the assault battalions crossed with little loss. The big mine under the Tambour position destroyed a number of dugouts and machine-guns and the advance pressed on.

The 7th Division assaulted towards Mametz and in spite of heavy casualties had, in fifteen minutes, reached the outskirts of the village. Enemy resistance at Mametz was less than fierce, and many prisoners were taken, although as usual the isolated machine-gun in a dugout inflicted heavy casualties. As the advance continued, enemy resistance stiffened until the advance was checked at Danzig Alley, a German trench north-west of Mametz, while counter-attacks developed from Mametz itself. The advantage of good liasion came in here, for the artillery barrage came back again to strafe the German positions, and with the arrival of reinforcements the advance continued. Moreover XIII Corp to the south were doing even better and the German positions in front of XV Corp were being outflanked. By mid-afternoon most of Mametz was in British hands.

German recovery was, as usual, rapid. Machine-guns which had survived the explosions of the Tambour mine came into action, slaughtering the 10th Yorkshires, including the Commanding Officer and his staff, and isolating the most forward companies. The West

Yorks lost twenty-two officers and six hundred and eighty-eight men during the day.

The 4th Middlesex Regiment was swept by concentrated fire from six machine-guns, and lost all their officers and all but forty men. The machine-gunning from Fricourt was of great intensity, and it was in the teeth of this, and at the cost of heavy losses, that the infantry brigades of the 21st Division forced their way into the German posts north of Fricourt, and fought with grenade and bayonet up and into the heart of the German trench system on the south side of Sausage Valley. The losses of Commanding Officers in particular were very heavy but the line was advancing and by 11 a.m. the British held the German positions around the sunken road, due north of Fricourt.

Throughout the day communications on the battle-field had been very difficult. The main means of communication in 1916 was by field telephone, which operated on wire land-lines laid by signallers. Attempts to bring telephone wire forward across No Man's Land failed, and the wire laid up to the Old Front Line, although laid in trenches some two feet deep, had frequently been cut by shell-fire. To report back the assault battalions had to use runners. Many of these were killed and others got lost. For all, the difficulties of getting back across the shell-torn fire-swept ground, along trenches choked with wounded and reinforcements

proved difficult, and as a result, divisional commanders
were very much in the dark as to the actual situation
at the front. In the absence of factual report, rumour
flourished and, not unnaturally, the more optimistic
reports were preferred and believed. It was in the
belief that he was building on an existing success far
greater than that actually achieved, that General
Horne, commanding XV Corp, ordered the main assault
on Fricourt.

The line of this assault was up a valley which
contained a riverlet called the Willow Stream. This
stream roughly divided the areas of the two assault
divisions of the XV Corp, both of which were to
combine for this, the third and final phase of the
Corp attack. The attack began in the early afternoon
and although some small gains were made, the casualties
were huge ; the Germans standing up on their parapets
to fire into the advancing British. Whole lines fell
together. The Green Howards lost fifteen officers and
three hundred and thirty-six men in the first three
minutes of the advance. By early evening the attack
had petered out, and along the Corp's front the
battalions concentrated on consolidating their gains
and digging in.

Overall, although Fricourt still held out, XV Corp
had done very well. Mametz had fallen and Fricourt
was outflanked. Only in the centre had there been

total failure, and although the Corp had lost seven thousand five hundred men, unlike the units to the north, it had at least something to show for it.

The last Corp in the 4th Army, the XIII, held the extreme right of the British line adjoining the French. The objective of XIII Corp was Montauban, and they took it. On their right the French were totally successful and took all their objectives for the day ; the reason for this should be analysed. For a start XIII Corp artillery when combined as it was with that of the French XX Corp, had more heavy guns than any other sector, and had already battered the German line before the assault began. Infantry and artillery co-operation was excellent.

It was here that the ''creeping barrage'' was first employed, invented by a Brigade Major of the 18th Divisional Artillery, Captain Alan Brooke, later to be Field-Marshal Lord Alanbrooke, Chief of the Imperial General Staff. In this the heavy artillery fire moves back in regular steps from one enemy position to the next. Between the heavy gun barrage and the advancing infantry the field artillery and mortars plaster the ground, and the infantry, as close up to this as safety allows, wait for the barrage to move, and then follow it. The effect is to keep the enemy's head down until the infantry are right on top of him. The wire on this front had been well cut, and the enemy trenches and deep dugouts had been largely destroyed. Moreover the advancing infantry mopped up as they went along, leaving no pockets of enemy to attack them later from the rear, or shoot up the supporting reserves as had happened elsewhere with disastrous results.

XIII Corp sent two divisions, the 30th and the 18th, into the assault. The Corp lost six thousand men, but by midday had taken all their objectives and their front was quiet again. The 30th Division advanced a mile and a quarter and, what is more important, stayed there, on a frontage of over a mile. The French, on their right, had also achieved all they had set out to do. They had more and heavier guns, and, south of the Somme, had waited until 9.30, two hours after the British, before attacking and thereby achieving complete surprise. They were also extremely efficient, and at the end of the day had taken over four thousand prisoners and all their objectives at comparatively little cost to themselves.

July 1, 1916, was the blackest day in the history of the British Army. Casualties totalled over fifty-seven thousand men, about 60 per cent of the attacking troops involved. Apart from the gains made by the two Corps nearest the French, and the French themselves, nothing was gained. As had been shown, the losses of the first day were due to a number of factors, and many of these could have been foreseen.

The nature of the ground, the deep dugouts, the lack of heavy guns, the belts of wire, the machine-guns, the efficiency of the German Army, the lack of training and poor communications of the British, all these, and other smaller and by themselves insignificant factors contributed to the worst disaster to British Armies since Hastings.

But July 1 was only the first day. The battle went on for another four and a half months, and the casualties and horrors rose with every passing day. The main features of the rest of the battle were the introduction of Dominion troops to the Western Front, and that great hope of the armies, the machine-gun-proof tank. As we shall see, events frustrated both the vigour of the Dominions, and the ingenuity of the tank. The losses of the rest of the Somme battle stem largely from what happened on July 1.

On the evening of that fatal day the front was comparatively quiet again. Everywhere men were working, to bring up supplies, to repair defences and to dig in. The wounded and dead were being removed from the wire, and the Generals were trying to discover the true situation and decide what to do about it. The ground behind the German line was thinly held. There is no doubt that the Generals in the south instead of consolidating their gains, should have scraped up every man and gun they could find and set them

forward to push on the advance. Patrols which had
been out had established that the woods and copses in
front of XV and XIII Corps were lightly held. They
should have been occupied before the Germans reinforced them. The day's gains were consolidated and
through their field glasses the battalion officers surveyed
the ground to their front, over which they must soon
advance. There, they established was Guillemont, and
that other village must be Ginchy. Over there lay
Trônes Wood and that one behind it must be Delville
Wood, with the village of Longueval along its western
side, and that other big wood on the skyline, that was
what the French called Bois de Fourneaux, and the
British, High Wood.

July 2nd–Nov. 18th, 1916

It would be a dulling repetition of horrors to describe
every action of the next four months. The battle
went on, and one day's fighting merged into another.
Only the highlights emerge with any real significance.
One of these highlights, and one which will illustrate
the fighting, was the large-scale introduction of the
Dominion forces to the Western Front. The Canadians
had been in France almost from the beginning. They
had a formidable reputation as fighting men, and had
almost alone resisted the panic caused by the first

German gas attack in 1915 and were to go on to later
fame with their exploits around Vimy Ridge in 1917.
The Canadians had introduced the trench raid, small
night attacks in anything up to battalion strength on
the German line, to kill, take prisoners, and wreck
trenches and dugouts. Divisional staffs became very
keen on raiding and, as the fashion spread, were
continually urging their front-line battalions to attack
the German line. This Canadian innovation was viewed
with mixed feelings by the allies, but the Canadians
themselves were valued and respected soldiers. We
have already noted how the Newfoundland Regiment
conducted itself at Beaumont Hamel.

The Anzac forces, from Australia and New Zealand,
had previously been in action at Gallipoli and prior to
July 1916 had not fought on the Western Front. The
South African Brigade of four battalions with support
arms, lay in reserve before the Somme battle, and
numbered in its ranks many men who had fought
against the British in the Boer War, sixteen years
before. There is no doubt that this South African
brigade had no superior among all the Dominion or
Colonial contingents fighting for Great Britain. Lacking something of the dash of the Australians, it
harnessed instead the solid, stolid reliability that the
Dutch element brought to the character of the men.
The adventurous streak in all Englishmen's make-up

came from the predominantly English population of
Natal, where the incredible hardships suffered by their
Dutch ancestors who had taken part in the Great Trek
only eighty years before, had implanted an amazing
ability to suffer the cruel conditions of Delville Wood
so valiantly. Other Empire troops, notably Indian
Cavalry were also in reserve, waiting for the expected
breakthrough.

After the losses of July 1 and the failure in so many
cases to achieve even the most minor objectives, one
has to wonder why the battle was not halted. Probably
the chance to halt the battle on July 2, or at least
switch the weight of attack to the south, was lost
because communications were poor, and before the true
picture had emerged, the attack went on again along
the entire front. As it began, so it continued, and
that this was a grave and forseeable error cannot be
doubted. The attack continued as originally planned
with assaults along the entire front, and a battle of
attrition was the inevitable outcome. General Gough
who had been building up a Reserve Army to exploit
the breakthrough was, on the evening of July 1, given
the command of the two northern Corps, the X and
the VIII. This Reserve Army became the 5th Army.

General Joffre chose this moment after the failure of
the initial assault to interfere, ordering Haig to attack
again in the centre, and although Haig, rightly, intended

to concentrate his efforts on the right flank, he could not assume that the French would support him. Nonetheless, an attack on the right flank was planned and executed on the night of July 13. In spite of the French lamentations that a night attack could never succeed, and that confusion would reign and disaster follow, the attack on Trônes Wood by XIII Corp was a complete success, and by dawn XIII not only had Trônes Wood but had occupied Longueval and held the south side of Delville Wood.

Taking a position was one thing, holding it another. The machine-gun was now yielding paramount position in the battlefield to the artillery piece. The woods and valleys were ranged to an inch and the shell storm that descended on these areas was awesome to behold and frightful to endure. As the fighting moved around Delville Wood, the South African Brigade was ordered forward.

Delville Wood is shaped rather like a right-angled triangle, choked with thick undergrowth and laced with barbed wire. Snipers flourished, and the wide rides with which the wood is crossed were enfiladed by machine guns.

On July 15, the South Africans attacked and took all but the northern tip of the wood. They held Delville Wood virtually unsupported for six days, under continuous shelling that at times reached the rate of four hundred shells a minute. They beat off counter-attack, machine-gun fire and sniping. Conditions in the wood were ghastly in the extreme. Shelling in woods is always bad. The shells are detonated by contact with the branches and tree trunks as they descend, spraying shrapnel directly into the trenches below. The undergrowth catches fire, burning the wounded as they lie unable to move, and as more and more trees are felled and the ground churned up by the shelling, the wood became a slaughterhouse. And it rained. With the rain came mud. Somme veterans talk at length about the mud. The Somme mud was the worst of the war. Chalk based, it was sticky, it could suck your boots off, and formed into great balls on your boots, making every movement an effort. Men drowned in it. In this charnal house of great and minor horrors the South Africans hung on. When they were relieved, only one hundred and forty-three men were still combatant. The Brigade had advanced to Delville Wood with one hundred and twenty-one officers and over three thousand men. Even when all elements were later gathered together, the Brigade totalled only seven hundred and fifty men, less than a single battalion.

High Wood lies behind Delville Wood, between Flers and Martinpuich, and overlooks all the surrounding countryside. The wood actually straddles the crest of a ridge so that the northern edge is on a reverse slope. In mid July, while the South Africans were fighting in Delville Wood, events were developing that made High Wood another black spot on the battlefield. It was believed by the local commanders that High Wood was unoccupied, and as the cavalry were to hand, and still uncommited on July 14, the 2nd Cavalry Division were ordered forward to take it. There were delays, and it was evening before the Cavalry arrived, but they went straight into action, and for a moment it seemed that glory and movement had indeed returned to the Western Front.

In long lines the Indian Cavalry (a Brigade consisting of the British 7th Dragoon Guards and the Indian Deccan Horse), lances and sabres flashing, charged up to the wood. In support, two English country battalions were coming up. The Germans were waiting, and the charge withered under the machine-guns. These two Cavalry Regiments had one hundred and two men hit, some fatally, while one hundred and thirty horses became casualties, mostly killed. It was not until seven weeks later that High Wood was at last in British hands. On July 17, Ovillers finally fell, a day or two after the garrison of La Boisselle had at last surrendered.

On the main axis of advance up the Baupaume Road, attention now shifted to Pozières. The village had been assaulted before, without success, as the position on the crest of a ride gave perfect visibility, and offered no cover to assaulting troops.

General Gough, commanding this sector of the battle, took the Anzac Corp under command, and directed General Birdwood, the Officer Commanding, to mount an attack against Pozières. On the 23rd, after scanty preparations, the attack began. The Australians fought for Pozières for six weeks and finally took it. The fighting was among the heaviest of the whole battle and the dead lay thicker around the Pozières windmill than anywhere else on the Somme, the Anzac Corp suffering twenty-three thousand casualties. The Australians were superb troops. The blooding they had received at Anzac in Gallipoli had hardened them to warfare, and no troops from the Dominions or Colonies had more active service ''know-how.'' They could not be stopped in the attack and the Germans feared them greatly. The Australian and Canadian Divisions retained their quality right up to the Armistice of 1918 and G.H.Q. came to rely on them more and more. This retention of quality, so sadly lacking in 1917 and 1918 in the ordinary British Divisions, was due firstly to the fact that all their brigades retained four battalions to the end, whereas the British brigades had to be reduced to three battalions owing to casualties and the difficulty of finding reinforcements, and secondly, that the superb quality of manhood in the

Dominions to replace their heavy casualties seemed to be maintained permanently. Their morale rarely sank and quickly recovered after a set-back.

On the other flank opposite Pozières, lay the village of Guillemont, only a few hundred yards north of Trônes Wood, on the top of a slope. To cross that distance and climb that slope took two months and great loss of life, but at last Guillemont and Pozières were taken and the British line, which had bulged and sagged was, by September 3, straight again, and a fresh major assault could be planned. September 15 was the date set, and to the aid of the assault was coming a new weapon as revolutionary as gunpowder itself, the tank.

The caterpillar-tracked vehicle had been known since the early years of the century, and the ability of such vehicles to cross rough ground had interested the War Office as far back as 1905. The initial interest had waned, and although cars, covered with boiler plate armour against machine-gun bullets were used outside Antwerp in 1914, the idea of putting an armoured vehicle on caterpillar tracks does not seem to have occurred to anyone until early in 1915, when Winston Churchill was approached to sponsor the idea of a tracked armoured fighting vehicle. Initial trials were only moderately successful, but in spite of War Office indifference, and the fact that Churchill's official position was First Sea Lord at the Admiralty, and nothing to do with the Army at all, he called the new prototypes "Landships" and gave them every support. The man actually working on the landships was Lt.-Col. E. D. Swinton, who became father of the tank, and eventually he persuaded the War Office to look again at the improved landship. Further and more successful trials followed, and in May 1916, two months before the Somme battle opened, the "Heavy Section, Machine Gun Corp" as the first tank unit was called, was formed at Grantham in Lincolnshire. The new machines were known as tanks very early on, as they were described as "tanks"—i.e. water tanks, to explain away their shrouded shapes on the way up to battle. The name was formally adopted in 1917, when the Tank Corps came into official existence. To-day it is the Royal Tank Regiment.

Haig, once convinced of the usefulness of this weapon, called for it urgently, but it was only a small force, barely trained, of fifty tanks that prepared to assist in the breakthrough towards Baupaume on September 15. The plan was to use them to spearhead an assault on a three-mile front ar und the villages of Flers and Courcelette. On the morning of September 15, the first tanks, moving in small detachments, rumbled forward among the infantry. They had a remarkable effect on the Germans.

Seven tanks attacked Flers in support of the New Zealand infantry. Four were hit and disabled by shell-fire, but the other three trundled on, over the wire and machine-gun posts, knocking down houses, cheered on by the delighted infantry. By the afternoon the tanks had helped in the capture of Courcelette and Martinpuich, and their success was the talk of the Armies. But there was not enough of them. They had been used in penny-packets, and while their initial appearance had surprised and terrified the enemy, the Germans had with typical resilience, risen to the challenge and turned their field guns on the tanks, with considerable effect. The initial surprise, that could have had an overwhelming effect had a larger number been used, was thrown away. For all that, September 15 and the Battle of Flers-Courcelette is a memorable day in the history of warfare.

The Canadians had been in action since early July, around Thiepval, relieving the Australians after the fall of Pozières. They supported the tank attack at Courcelette on September 15, and were still in the line when the Battle of the Somme officially ended in November. To the Somme front came battalions of every regiment in the British Army, some of them more than once. As they were used up, they were refilled with fresh recruits and returned to the line to fight again.

Finally, on November, 18 the offensive ended. It had effectively stopped some days before, for the Autumn rains had arrived early, and turned the battlefield into a sea of mud in which movement was all but impossible. The final actions took place on the now notorious Albert–Baupaume road, near the village of La Sars, under the eye of the Butte de Warlencourt, a Gallic burial mound some sixty feet high. All green trees and cover had been blasted from the Butte, which stood like a huge white tombstone towering over the battlefield, and on November 13, the Durham Light Infantry went over and occupied it. The last battle of the Somme was over.

During the winter the two armies lay in the frozen mud, glowering at each other unable to move, until one day, in the early spring of 1917, the Germans had gone. Silently, the Germans had withdrawn to the Hindenburg Line in front of Cambrai, a new fortified position they had spent the winter preparing. Behind them as they withdrew the countryside lay barren. They scorched the earth, burned and destroyed everything behind them, and booby traps and delayed action mines were left to meet the British as they hesitantly advanced over the deserted land. Picking up a bottle, moving a chair, stepping on a duck-board would set a mine off.

In the bibliography the reader will find listed books

that will explain in many ways and much detail all that happened on the Somme.

The Somme is generally remembered, if at all, as a hopeless battle, which achieved nothing. This is not true.

It is also generally believed that while the men suffered and died at the front, the Generals and the staff stayed in their châteaux drinking champagne and disregarding facts too unpleasant to believe. This is not true either. Divisional Generals were often in the Front Line. Brigade staff were usually well forward under fire. It is only at Corps and Army level that the Generals grew remote from events. But remoteness and indifference are not the same.

Hindsight is a gift of which most men are possessed. It is only by approaching the difficulties and problems as they appeared at the time that a fair judgement can be made. Haig as a commander has been much maligned, and yet it is difficult to see what else he could have done in the circumstances. Warfare is at best a chancy business in which the unexpected and the accidental often combine to defeat even the best laid plans.

The Somme achieved positive gains. It destroyed the German Field Army. It relieved Verdun—where German attacks had been going on for five months. They ceased eleven days after the Somme offensive started. The retreat of the Germans pushed their lines back almost to Cambrai, and the extra distance was used by the British to absorb the last great German offensive, over the same ground, in March 1918.

But the battle cost the British nation half a million men, a huge figure and one that cannot be shrugged off. Too many men were lost in attacks that continued long after they had become pointless, and the last word on such actions lies with Basil Liddell Hart.

''To throw good money after bad is foolish. But to throw away men's lives where there is no reasonable chance of advantage, is criminal. In the heat of the battle mistakes in the command are inevitable and amply excusable. But the real fault of leadership arises when attacks that are inherently vain are ordered merely because if they could succeed they would be useful. For such manslaughter, whether it springs from ignorance, a false conception of war or a want of moral courage, commanders should be held accountable to the nation.''

CHAPTER III

THE BATTLEFIELD TO-DAY

Most battles, lamented one General, are fought at the junction of two maps, and so it is with the Somme. The intending visitor should first equip himself with maps of a minimum scale of 1–50,000, published by the French Institute Geographique National, and obtainable, eventually, from any U.K. agent of the Ordnance Survey. The visitor will require two, those for Baupaume and Albert, which can be joined on the point where the Albert–Baupaume road runs off the Albert map at Poziers, after which the outline of the Old Front Line can be marked upon it. Thus equipped, and possessing at least some of the books suggested in the bibliography, the traveller's tour may commence. The woods and villages are mostly still there, and to a surprising extent ''all as it was.'' The best way is to mark the map and wander.

Most visitors would chose to stay in Amiens, fourteen miles from the battlefield. Amiens is a large modern town, well equipped with comfortable hotels and restaurants. It also contains the famous Godbert Restaurant, in the Rue des Jacobins, written about by Sassoon, and Williamson, and other soldier writers of the Somme. Many British Officers dined there, when having a day off. It is still very good.

The road out to Albert takes the motorist past Amiens prison, scene of the famous R.A.F. attack in World War II. In the prison were a number of British officers who had been captured after being parachuted behind the German lines. Their knowledge of the state of the retreating German army would be invaluable and the approach of Montgomery's 21st Army Group suggested that these officers might very reasonably be transferred deep into Germany. Speed and highly accurate bombing was necessary, available and successful. The lighter bricks mark the outline of the repair to the breach the flyers made in the wall of that grim Gestapo prison.

About eight miles from Amiens the road passes through the village of Querrieu, where General Rawlinson sited his 4th Army Headquarters. The gates of the château are to the left on entering the village. On leaving it, past the little war memorial, the visitor looking back over his left shoulder will see the garden façade, and the steps on which King George V, Sir Douglas Haig and General Rawlinson met in 1916. The road heads straight for Albert, rising and falling

over the downland until, cresting the rise one can see
on the skyline a figure gleaming and glittering in the
sun. The Golden Virgin of Albert is welcoming the
visitor to the battlefield.

To anyone knowing anything of the battle, having
read the books and heard the stories, there is something
startling in the first sight of the Golden Virgin ; for
more than any other single place or monument, this
is the symbol of the Somme. In 1915, a shell struck
the Campanile of Albert Cathedral, bending the steel
girder that held the statue until the figure hung out
over the square below. Thousands of British soldiers
marched under the Virgin on their way up to the
batttlefield, and legends grew up about her. The
inhabitants of Albert, and most of the British troops
working permanently in the town, believed that when
the Virgin finally fell the war would end and the Allies
defeated. The French, taking no chances, fixed the
statue in position with steel cables. There she hung
until 1918 when another shell sent her crashing into
the square below, and in 1918 it was the Germans who
were defeated. In 1927, the Virgin was replaced on
the basilica, and there she is to-day, holding the Christ
Child triumphantly aloft, to view the countryside to
which peace has been restored. She can be seen from
many points on the battlefield, gleaming in the sunshine.

Generally, the countryside has recovered well from

the blast of war. The poppies, which thrive on chalk, grow in great profusion and yellowhammers start from the hedgerows just as the soldiers remember them.

Apart from the odd mine crater, a trench outline, some fields curiously uneven from the dents of old shell holes, the Somme is at first glance like any other peaceful place. But as the ground becomes familiar, the unobtrusive marks of war are many. Most obvious of all are the cemeteries, all beautifully preserved by the Commonwealth War Graves Commission. Each cemetery contains a register, giving details of the actions fought about that spot, and listing the names and regiments of those who lie buried there, with accurate details regarding the precise position of each grave. Any one of them can be found in a few minutes. The Great Monument of Thiepval lists over seventy thousand Allied missing, who have no known grave.

Surprisingly, there is only one German Cemetery on the battlefield, at Fricourt, a stark flowerless place, containing some 5,000 dead. No one seems to know what happened to the rest. Perhaps the German dead were shipped home to Germany, but most probably they were simply buried in unmarked graves, long since obliterated. Perhaps these are the bodies that are found on the battlefield every year. Next to the graveyards, the most noticeable sights are the mine craters.

The "Y" Sap and Lochnager craters are on either side of La Boisselle, the Y Sap just beside the main road. To reach Lochnager, the motorist should drive up a narrow road off to the right, noting the tumbled ground of the "Glory Hole" on either side, until he comes to the "Grande Mine." It is an enormous crater, one hundred feet wide and sixty feet deep ; so large that trees grow comfortably in the bottom. It is by far the most imposing on the Old Front Line. The Hawthorn Ridge crater, above Beaumont Hame, is much overgrown and choked with undergrowth, while the Tambour mines around Fricourt are now well wired off, to keep out cattle and, at the same time, tourists.

There has only been one attempt to preserve a part of the Old Front Line on the Somme, up by Auchonvillers, where the Canadian Government have a memorial park to the Newfoundland Regiment. Here the visitor can walk among the wire stakes, over the ground down which the Newfoundlanders charged to their deaths, and one can sit in the positions from which the machine-guns raked them. Taking the car along the road from Hamel to Auchonvillers and then leaving it at the 29th Divisional Memorial, an easy walk with map and binoculars, will result in the visitor finding relics everywhere. He is walking into history. The hollows in the sides of banks mark the entrances to old

dugouts, now collapsed. The white splotches in the
fields mark the old trench lines, while the fields themselves are usually fenced in with wire supported on
old curly trench screw pickets, salvaged from the
battlefield.

Underfoot come further curiosities. An unexploded
shell, white with chalk, lies beside the plough furrows,
and the visitor should leave it there. The plough every
year brings up shells, bullets, broken rifles, heaps of
shrapnel. A rusting helmet adorns a scarecrow, two
5.9 shells, freshly painted, top the gateposts of a farm.
After the war, the regiments erected monuments to
their dead all over the battlefield, indeed all over the
Western Front, and the visitor will find these at every
turn. Delville Wood is now laid out as a memorial to
the gallant South Africans, many of whom lie buried
in the graveyard opposite the wood. High Wood,
dark and menacing again, dripping with moisture and
choked with undergrowth, is as grim as ever. The
ground within, as in all the woods on the Somme, is
dented with shell holes, and the rubbish of old dugouts.
Green slimy shells are found in little dumps under the
trees. The woods about the Somme are dismal places.
They should only be entered with care and no shells
or bombs touched. They are still dangerous. The
villages might never have been destroyed. They were
rebuilt on the old foundations, standing exactly as

before. Fricourt and Mametz, Ovillers and Le Sars stand just as if the war had by-passed them.

Past Le Sars, on the right of the Albert–Baupaume road, stands the Butte de Warlencourt. It looks to-day like a bunch of trees, and it is not until the undergrowth at the bottom is entered that the rising earth of the old Gallic mound can be located and climbed. On the top, among the scrub is an old wooden cross, and from the Butte the traveller can look back over the battlefield, down the straight road to Pozières and Albert, across a countryside studded with cemeteries and the lost graves of a generation. In front of the Butte, in the freezing wet November of 1916, the great Somme offensive finally petered out, halted by mud and exhaustion. Looking down from the Butte to-day, at the cars and caravans streaming along the road below it hardly seems possible, and perhaps this is why people visit the battlefields.

For a battlefield is, at the end, a piece of ground. It is the battle and the men that fought it who gave the ground significance. The visitor can only wonder if he himself could have endured as much there.

''It couldn't be done again,'' wrote Fitzgerald.
''This Western Front business couldn't be done
again, not for a long time. The young men think
they could do it again, but they couldn't. This took
religion and years of plenty and tremendous sureties
and the exact relation that existed between the
classes''

No, it couldn't be done again. Even if man were so
foolish, modern arms—aerial, nuclear, mechanical
would make it impossible, and it is certain that trench
warfare will only be experienced once in the whole
history of the world.

BIBLIOGRAPHY

The following books are readily obtainable from book-shops or libraries :

Official Histories : *Military Operations, France and Belgium, 1916*, Vols. 5 and 6.   Pub : H.M.S.O.

Private Papers of Douglas Haig.   Robert Blake, 1952.

The Somme.   Anthony Farrar Hockley.   Pub : Pan Books.

The Ironclads of Cambrai.   Bryan Cooper.   Pub : Pan Books, 1967.

The Golden Virgin.   Henry Williamson.   Pub : MacDonald.

Soldier from the Wars Returning.   C. E. Carrington.   Pub : Panther, 1970.

Memoirs of an Infantry Officer.   Siegfried Sassoon.   Pub : Faber.

Goodbye to All That.   Robert Graves.   Pub : Penguin.

Undertones of War.   Edmund Blunden.   Pub : Penguin.

Passionate Prodigality.   Guy Chapman.   Pub : Peter Davies.

Saggitarius Rising. Cecil Lewis. Pub : Peter Davies.
The First Day on the Somme. Martin Middlebrook.
Pub : Penguin, 1970.
The Price of Glory. Alistair Horne. Pub : Macmillan,
1962.

The following books may need to be ordered :

Trekking On. Lt. Col. Denys Reitz.
A Subalterns War. C. E. Edmonds. Pub : Library
Association.
A Subaltern on the Somme. " Mark VII."
Up to Mametz. L. W. Griffith.
History of the World War. Basil Liddel Hart.

Histories of the Commonwealth Troops, or of British
Regiments can be studied in the Library of the
Imperial War Museum.

THE OLD FRONT LINE

CHAPTER I

THIS description of the old front line, as it was when the Battle of the Somme began, may some day be of use. All wars end; even this war will some day end, and the ruins will be rebuilt and the field full of death will grow food, and all this frontier of trouble will be forgotten. When the trenches are filled in, and the plough has gone over them, the ground will not long keep the look of war. One summer with its flowers will cover most of the ruin that man can make, and then these places, from which the driving back of the enemy began, will be hard indeed to trace, even with maps. It is said that even now in some places the wire has been removed, the explosive salved, the trenches filled, and the ground ploughed with tractors. In a few years' time, when this war is a romance in memory, the soldier looking for his battlefield will find his marks gone. Centre Way, Peel Trench, Munster Alley, and these other paths to glory will be deep under the corn, and gleaners will sing at Dead Mule Corner.

75

It is hoped that this description of the line will be followed by an account of our people's share in the battle. The old front line was the base from which the battle proceeded. It was the starting-place. The thing began there. It was the biggest battle in which our people were ever engaged, and so far it has led to bigger results than any battle of this war since the Battle of the Marne. It caused a great falling back of the enemy armies. It freed a great tract of France, seventy miles long, by from ten to twenty-five miles broad. It first gave the enemy the knowledge that he was beaten.

Very many of our people never lived to know the result of even the first day's fighting. For them the old front line was the battlefield, and the No Man's Land the prize of the battle. They never heard the cheer of victory nor looked into an enemy trench. Some among them never even saw the No Man's Land, but died in the summer morning from some shell in the trench in the old front line here described.

It is a difficult thing to describe without monotony, for it varies so little. It is like describing the course of the Thames from Oxford to Reading, or of the Severn from Deerhurst to Lydney, or of the Hudson from New York to Tarrytown. Whatever country the rivers pass they remain water, bordered by shore. So our front-line trenches, wherever they lie, are only gashes in the earth, fenced by wire, beside a greenish strip of ground, pitted with shell-holes, which is fenced with thicker, blacker, but more tumbled wire on the other side. Behind this further wire is the parapet of the enemy front-line trench, which swerves to take in a hillock or to flank a dip, or to crown a slope, but remains roughly parallel with ours, from seventy to five hundred yards from it, for miles and miles, up hill and down dale. All the advantages of position and observation were in the enemy's hands, not in ours. They took up their lines when they were strong and our side weak, and in no place in all the old Somme position is our line better sited than theirs, though in one or two places the sites are nearly equal. Almost in every part of this old front our men had to go up hill to attack.

If the description of this old line be dull to read, it should be remembered that it was dull to hold. The enemy had the lookout posts, with the fine views over France, and the sense of domination. Our men were down below with no view of anything but of stronghold after stronghold, just up above, being made stronger daily. And if the enemy had strength of position he had also strength of equipment, of men, of guns, and explosives of all kinds. He had all the advantages for nearly two years of war, and in all that time our old front line, whether held by the French or by ourselves, was nothing but a post to be endured, day in day out, in all weathers and under all fires, in doubt, difficulty, and danger, with bluff and makeshift and improvisation, till the tide could be turned. If it be dull to read about and to see, it was, at least, the old line which kept back the tide and stood the siege. It was the line from which, after all those months of war, the tide turned and the besieged became the attackers.

To most of the British soldiers who took part in the Battle of the Somme, the town of Albert must be a central point in a reckoning of distances. It lies, roughly speaking, behind the middle of the line of that battle. It is a knot of roads, so that supports and supplies could and did move from it to all parts of the line during the battle. It is on the main road, and on the direct railway line from Amiens. It is by much the most important town within an easy march of the battle-field. It will be, quite certainly, the centre from which, in time to come, travellers will start to see the battle-field where such deeds were done by men of our race.

It is not now (after three years of war and many bombardments) an attractive town; probably it never was. It is a small straggling town built of red brick along a knot of cross-roads at a point where the swift chalk-river Ancre, hardly more than a brook, is bridged

and so channelled that it can be used for power.   Before
the war it contained a few small factories, including one
for the making of sewing-machines.   Its most important building was a big church built a few years ago,
through the energy of a priest, as a shrine for the
Virgin of Albert, a small, probably not very old image,
about which strange stories are told.   Before the war it
was thought that this church would become a northern
rival to Lourdes for the working of miraculous cures
during the September pilgrimage.   A gilded statue of
the Virgin and Child stood on an iron stalk on the
summit of the church tower.   During a bombardment
of the town at a little after three o'clock in the afternoon of Friday, January 15, 1915, a shell so bent the
stalk that the statue bent down over the Place as though
diving.   Perhaps few of our soldiers will remember
Albert for anything except this diving Virgin.   Perhaps
half of the men engaged in the Battle of the Somme
passed underneath her as they marched up to the line,
and, glancing up, hoped that she might not come down
till they were past.   From someone, French or English,
a word has gone about that when she does fall the war
will end.   Others have said that French engineers have
so fixed her with wire ropes that she cannot fall.

From Albert four roads lead to the battlefield of the
Somme :

1. In a north-westerly direction to Auchonvillers and Hébuterne.

2. In a northerly direction to Authuille and Hamel.

3. In a north-easterly direction to Pozières.

4. In an easterly direction to Fricourt and Maricourt.

Between the second and the third of these the little river Ancre runs down its broad, flat, well-wooded valley, much of which is a marsh through which the river (and man) have forced more than one channel. This river, which is a swift, clear, chalk stream, sometimes too deep and swift to ford, cuts the English sector of the battlefield into two nearly equal portions.

Following the first of the four roads, one passes the wooded village of Martinsart, to the village of Auchonvillers, which lies among a clump of trees upon a ridge or plateau top. The road dips here, but soon rises again, and so, by a flat tableland, to the large village of Hébuterne. Most of this road, with the exception of one little stretch near Auchonvillers, is hidden by high ground from every part of the battlefield. Men moving upon it cannot see the field.

Hébuterne, although close to the line and shelled daily and nightly for more than two years, was never the object of an attack in force, so that much of it remains. Many of its walls and parts of some of its roofs still stand, the church tower is in fair order, and no one walking in the streets can doubt that he is in a village. Before the war it was a prosperous village ; then, for more than two years, it rang with the roar of battle and with the business of an army. Presently the tide of the war ebbed away from it and left it deserted, so that one may walk in it now, from end to end, without seeing a human being. It is as though the place had been smitten by the plague. Villages during the Black Death must have looked thus. One walks in the village expecting at every turn to meet a survivor, but there is none ; the village is dead ; the grass is growing in the street ; the bells are silent ; the beasts are gone from the byre and the ghosts from the church. Stealing about among the ruins and the gardens are the cats of the village, who have eaten too much man to fear him, but are now too wild to come to him. They creep about and eye him from cover and look like evil spirits.

The second of the four roads passes out of Albert, crosses the railway at a sharp turn, over a bridge called Marmont Bridge, and runs northward along the valley of the Ancre within sight of the railway. Just beyond the Marmont Bridge there is a sort of lake or reservoir or catchment of the Ancre overflows, a little to the right of the road. By looking across this lake as he walks northward, the traveller can see some rolls of gentle chalk hill, just beyond which the English front line ran at the beginning of the battle.

A little further on, at the top of a rise, the road passes the village of Aveluy, where there is a bridge or causeway over the Ancre valley. Aveluy itself, being within a mile and a half of enemy gun positions for nearly two years of war, is knocked about, and rather roofless and windowless. A cross-road leading to the causeway across the valley once gave the place some little importance.

Not far to the north of Aveluy, the road runs for more than a mile through the Wood of Aveluy, which is a well-grown plantation of trees and shrubs. This wood hides the marsh of the river from the traveller. Tracks from the road lead down to the marsh and across it by military causeways.

On emerging from the wood, the road runs within hail of the railway, under a steep and high chalk bank partly copsed with scrub. Three-quarters of a mile from the wood it passes through the skeleton of the village of Hamel, which is now a few ruined walls of brick standing in orchards on a hillside. Just north of this village, crossing the road, the railway, and the river-valley, is the old English front line.

The third of the four roads is one of the main roads of France. It is the state highway, laid on the line of a Roman road, from Albert to Bapaume. It is by far the most used and the most important of the roads crossing the battlefield. As it leads directly to Bapaume, which was one of the prizes of the victory, and points like a sword through the heart of the enemy positions it will stay in the memories of our soldiers as the main avenue of the battle.

The road leaves Albert in a street of dingy and rather broken red-brick houses. After passing a corner crucifix it shakes itself free of the houses and rises slowly up a ridge of chalk hill about three hundred feet high. On the left of the road, this ridge, which is much withered and trodden by troops and horses, is called Usna Hill. On the right, where the grass is green and the chalk of the old communication trenches still white and clean, it is called Tara Hill. Far away on the left, along the line of the Usna Hill, one can see the Aveluy Wood.

Looking northward from the top of the Usna-Tara Hill to the dip below it and along the road for a few yards up the opposite slope, one sees where the old English front line crossed the road at right angles. The enemy front line faced it at a few yards' distance, just about two miles from Albert town.

The fourth of the four roads runs for about a mile eastwards from Albert, and then slopes down into a kind of gully or shallow valley, through which a brook once ran and now dribbles. The road crosses the brook-course, and runs parallel with it for a little while to a place where the ground on the left comes down in a slanting tongue and on the right rises steeply into a big hill. The ground of the tongue bears traces of human habitation on it, all much smashed and discoloured. This is the once pretty village of Fricourt. The hill on the right front at this point is the Fricourt Salient. The lines run round the salient and the road cuts across them.

Beyond Fricourt, the road leaves another slanting tongue at some distance to its left. On this second tongue the village of Mametz once stood. Near here the road, having now cut across the salient, again crosses both sets of lines, and begins a long, slow ascent to a ridge or crest. From this point, for a couple of miles, the road is planted on each side with well-grown plane-trees, in some of which magpies have built their nests ever since the war began. At the top of the rise the road runs along the plateau top (under trees which show more and more plainly the marks of war) to a village so planted that it seems to stand in a wood. The village is built of red brick, and is rather badly broken by enemy shell fire, though some of the houses in it are still habitable. This is the village of Maricourt. Three or four hundred yards beyond Maricourt the road reaches the old English front line, at the eastern extremity of the English sector, as it was at the beginning of the battle.

CHAPTER II

THESE four roads which lead to the centre and the
wings of the battlefield were all, throughout the battle
and for the months of war which preceded it, dangerous
by daylight. All could be shelled by the map, and all,
even the first, which was by much the best hidden of
the four, could be seen, in places, from the enemy
position. On some of the trees or tree stumps by the
sides of the roads one may still see the "camouflage"
by which these exposed places were screened from the
enemy observers. The four roads were not greatly
used in the months of war which preceded the battle.
In those months, the front was too near to them, and
other lines of supply and approach were more direct
and safer. But there was always some traffic upon
them of men going into the line or coming out, of
ration parties, munition and water carriers, and ambu-
lances. On all four roads many men of our race were
killed. All, at some time, or many times, rang and
flashed with explosions. Danger, death, shocking

escape and firm resolve, went up and down those roads daily and nightly. Our men slept and ate and sweated and dug and died along them after all hardships and in all weathers. On parts of them, no traffic moved, even at night, so that the grass grew high upon them. Presently, they will be quiet country roads again, and tourists will walk at ease, where brave men once ran and dodged and cursed their luck, when the Battle of the Somme was raging.

Then, indeed, those roads were used. Then the grass that had grown on some of them was trodden and crushed under. The trees and banks by the waysides were used to hide batteries, which roared all day and all night. At all hours and in all weathers the convoys of horses slipped and stamped along those roads with more shells for the ever-greedy cannon. At night, from every part of those roads, one saw a twilight of summer lightning winking over the high ground from the never-ceasing flashes of guns and shells. Then there was no quiet, but a roaring, a crashing, and a screaming from guns, from shells bursting and from shells passing in the air. Then, too, on the two roads to the east of the Ancre River, the troops for the battle moved up to the line. The battalions were played by their bands through Albert, and up the slope of Usna Hill to Pozières and beyond, or past Fricourt and the wreck of Mametz to Montauban and the bloody woodland near it. Those roads then were indeed paths of glory leading to the grave.

During the months which preceded the Battle of the Somme, other roads behind our front lines were more used than these. Little villages, out of shell fire, some miles from the lines, were then of more use to us than Albert. Long after we are gone, perhaps, stray English tourists, wandering in Picardy, will see names scratched in a barn, some mark or notice on a door, some sign-post, some little line of graves, or hear, on the lips of a native, some slang phrase of English, learned long before in the war-time, in childhood, when the English were there. All the villages behind our front were thronged with our people. There they rested after being in the line and there they established their hospitals and magazines. It may be said, that men of our race died in our cause in every village within five miles of the front. Wherever the traveller comes upon a little company of our graves, he will know that he is near the site of some old hospital or clearing station, where our men were brought in from the line.

So much for the roads by which our men marched to this battlefield. Near the lines they had to leave the roads for the shelter of some communication trench or deep cut in the mud, revetted at the sides with wire to hinder it from collapsing inwards. By these deep narrow roads, only broad enough for marching in single file, our men passed to "the front," to the line itself. Here and there, in recesses in the trench, under roofs of corrugated iron covered with sandbags, they passed the offices and the stores of war, telephonists, battalion headquarters, dumps of bombs, barbed wire, rockets, lights, machine-gun ammunition, tins, jars, and cases. Many men, passing these things as they went "in" for the first time, felt with a sinking of the heart, that they were leaving all ordered and arranged things, perhaps for ever, and that the men in charge of these stores enjoyed, by comparison, a life like a life at home.

Much of the relief and munitioning of the fighting lines was done at night. Men going into the lines saw little of where they were going. They entered the gash of the communication trench, following the load on the back of the man in front, but seeing perhaps nothing but the shape in front, the black walls of the trench, and now and then some gleam of a star in the water under foot. Sometimes as they marched they would see the starshells, going up and bursting like rockets, and coming down with a wavering slow settling motion, as white and bright as burning magnesium wire, shedding a kind of dust of light upon the trench and making the blackness intense when they went out. These lights, the glimmer in the sky from the enemy's guns, and now and then the flash of a shell, were the things seen by most of our men on their first going in.

In the fire trench they saw little more than the parapet. If work were being done in the No Man's Land, they still saw little save by these lights that floated and fell from the enemy and from ourselves. They could see only an array of stakes tangled with wire, and something distant and dark which might be similar stakes, or bushes, or men, in front of what could only be the enemy line. When the night passed, and those working outside the trench had to take shelter, they could see nothing, even at a loophole or periscope, but the greenish strip of ground, pitted with shell-holes and fenced with wire, running up to the enemy line. There was little else for them to see, looking to the front, for miles and miles, up hill and down dale.

The soldiers who held this old front line of ours saw this grass and wire day after day, perhaps, for many months. It was the limit of their world, the horizon of their landscape, the boundary. What interest there was in their life was the speculation, what lay beyond that wire, and what the enemy was doing there. They seldom saw an enemy. They heard his songs and they were stricken by his missiles, but seldom saw more than, perhaps, a swiftly moving cap at a gap in the broken parapet, or a grey figure flitting from the light of a star-

shell. Aeroplanes brought back photographs of those
unseen lines. Sometimes, in raids in the night, our men
visited them and brought back prisoners; but they
remained mysteries and unknown.

In the early morning of the 1st of July, 1916, our
men looked at them as they showed among the bursts
of our shells. Those familiar heaps, the lines, were
then in a smoke of dust full of flying clods and shards
and gleams of fire. Our men felt that now, in a few
minutes, they would see the enemy and know what lay
beyond those parapets and probe the heart of that
mystery. So, for the last half-hour, they watched and
held themselves ready, while the screaming of the shells
grew wilder and the roar of the bursts quickened into a
drumming. Then as the time drew near, they looked a
last look at that unknown country, now almost blotted
in the fog of war, and saw the flash of our shells,
breaking a little further off as the gunners "lifted," and
knew that the moment had come. Then for one wild
confused moment they knew that they were running
towards that unknown land, which they could still see
in the dust ahead. For a moment, they saw the
parapet with the wire in front of it, and began, as they
ran, to pick out in their minds a path through that wire.
Then, too often, to many of them, the grass that they
were crossing flew up in shards and sods and gleams of
fire from the enemy shells, and those runners never

reached the wire, but saw, perhaps, a flash, and the earth rushing nearer, and grasses against the sky, and then saw nothing more at all, for ever and for ever and for ever.

It may be some years before those whose fathers, husband and brothers were killed in this great battle, may be able to visit the battlefield where their dead are buried. Perhaps many of them, from brooding on the map, and from dreams and visions in the night, have in their minds an image or picture of that place. The following pages may help some few others, who have not already formed that image, to see the scene as it appears to-day. What it was like on the day of battle cannot be imagined by those who were not there.

It was a day of an intense blue summer beauty, full of roaring, violence, and confusion of death, agony, and triumph, from dawn till dark. All through that day, little rushes of the men of our race went towards that No Man's Land from the bloody shelter of our trenches. Some hardly left our trenches, many never crossed the green space, many died in the enemy wire, many had to fall back. Others won across and went further, and drove the enemy from his fort, and then back from line to line and from one hasty trenching to another, till the Battle of the Somme ended in the falling back of the enemy army.

CHAPTER III

THOSE of our men who were in the line at Hébuterne, at the extreme northern end of the battlefield of the Somme, were opposite the enemy salient of Gommecourt. This was one of those projecting fortresses or flankers, like the Leipzig, Ovillers, and Fricourt, with which the enemy studded and strengthened his front line. It is doubtful if any point in the line in France was stronger than this point of Gommecourt. Those who visit it in future times may be surprised that such a place was so strong.

All the country there is gentler and less decided than in the southern parts of the batttlefield. Hébuterne stands on a plateau-top; to the east of it there is a gentle dip down to a shallow hollow or valley; to the east of this again there is a gentle rise to higher ground, on which the village of Gommecourt stood. The church of Gommecourt is almost exactly one mile north-east and by north from the church at Hébuterne; both churches being at the hearts of their villages.

Seen from our front line at Hébuterne, Gommecourt is little more than a few red-brick buildings, standing in woodland on a rise of ground. Wood hides the village to the north, the west, and the south-west. A big spur of woodland, known as Gommecourt Park, thrusts out boldly from the village towards the plateau on which the English lines stood. This spur, strongly fortified by the enemy, made the greater part of the salient in the enemy line. The landscape away from the wood is not in any way remarkable, except that it is open, and gentle, and on a generous scale. Looking north from our position at Hébuterne there is the snout of the woodland salient; looking south there is the green shallow shelving hollow or valley which made the No Man's Land for rather more than a mile. It is just such a gentle waterless hollow, like a dried-up river-bed, as one may see in several places in chalk country in England, but it is unenclosed land, and therefore more open and seemingly on a bigger scale than such a landscape would be in England, where most fields are small and fenced. Our old front line runs where the ground shelves or glides down into the valley; the enemy front line runs along the gentle rise up from the valley. The lines face each other across the slopes. To the south, the slope on which the enemy line stands is very slight.

The impression given by this tract of land once held by the enemy is one of graceful gentleness. The wood

on the little spur, even now, has something green about
it.   The village, once almost within the wood, wrecked
to shatters as it is, has still a charm of situation.   In
the distance behind Gommecourt there is some ill-
defined rising ground forming gullies and ravines.   On
these rises are some dark clumps of woodland, one of
them called after the nightingales, which perhaps sing
there this year, in what is left of their home.   There is
nothing now to show that this quiet landscape was one
of the tragical places of this war.

The whole field of the Somme is chalk hill and downland, like similar formations in England.   It has about
it, in every part of it, certain features well known to
everyone who has ever lived or travelled in a chalk
country.   These features occur even in the gentle,
rolling, and not strongly marked sector near Hébuterne.
Two are very noticeable, the formation almost everywhere of those steep, regular banks or terraces, which
the French call *remblais* and our own farmers lynchets,
and the presence, in nearly all parts of the field, of roads
sunken between two such banks into a kind of narrow
gully or ravine.   It is said, that these *remblais*, or
lynchets, which may be seen in English chalk countries,
as in the Dunstable Downs, in the Chiltern Hills, and
in many parts of Berkshire and Wiltshire, are made in
each instance, in a short time, by the ploughing away
from the top and bottom of any difficult slope.   Where

two slopes adjoin, such ploughing steepens the valley between them into a gully, which, being always unsown, makes a track through the crops when they are up. Sometimes, though less frequently, the farmer ploughs away from a used track on quite flat land, and by doing this on both sides of the track, he makes the track a causeway or ridgeway, slightly raised above the adjoining fields. This type of raised road or track can be seen in one or two parts of the battlefield (just above Hamel and near Pozieres, for instance), but the hollow or sunken road and the steep *remblai*, or lynchet, are everywhere. One may say that no quarter of a mile of the whole field is without one or other of them. The sunken roads are sometimes very deep. Many of our soldiers, on seeing them, have thought that they were cuttings made, with great labour, through the chalk, and that the *remblais*, or lynchets, were piled up and smoothed for some unknown purpose by primitive man. Probably it will be found, that in every case they are natural slopes made sharper by cultivation. Two or three of these lynchets and sunken roads cross the shallow valley of the No Man's Land near Hébuterne. By the side of one of them, a line of Sixteen Poplars, now ruined, made a landmark between the lines.

The line continues (with some slight eastward trendings, but without a change in its gentle quiet) southwards from this point for about a mile to a slight jut, or salient in the enemy line. This jut was known by our men as the Point, and a very spiky point it was to handle. From near the Point on our side of No Man's Land, a bank or lynchet, topped along its edge with trees, runs southwards for about a mile. In four places, the trees about this lynchet grow in clumps or copses, which our men called after the four Evangelists, John, Luke, Mark, and Matthew. This bank marks the old English front line between the Point and the Serre Road a mile to the south of it. Behind this English line are several small copses, on ground which very gently rises towards the crest of the plateau a mile to the west. In front of most of this part of our line, the ground rises towards the enemy trenches, so that one can see little to the front, but the slope up. The No Man's Land here is not green, but as full of shell-holes and the ruin of battle as any piece of the field. Directly between Serre and the Matthew Copse, where the lines cross a rough lump of ground, the enemy parapet is whitish from the chalk. The whitish parapet makes the skyline to observers in the Engish line. Over that parapet, some English battalions made one of the most splendid charges of the battle, in the heroic attack on Serre four hundred yards beyond.

To the right of our front at Matthew Copse the ground slopes southward a little, past what may once have been a pond or quarry, but is now a pit in the mud, to the

1. German deep dugout in Bernafay Wood 1916.

2. Bringing in a wounded man under fire at Beaumont Hamel. July 1st, 1916.

3. German trenches at Gommecourt.

4. Bringing a German gun out of High Wood, 1916.

5. "Observe the effect of shellfire," 1971.

6. Lochnager mine crater at La Boiselle, 1971.

7. Aveluy Wood, 1917.

8. Aveluy Wood, 1971.

9. The Deccan Horse before High Wood, July, 1916.

10. The Mill Road over the Ancre, 1916.

11. The Ancre, 1971, by the Mill Road.

12. The Golden Virgin of Albert.

13. Mk I tank crossing trench to attack Thiepval, September, 1916.

14. " Y " Ravine, 1967.

15. Towards the " Y " Ravine, 1971.

16. Butte de Warlencourt, 1971.

17. Australian Memorial at Pozières.

18. Butte de Warlencourt, 1918.

19. Sunken Jane : where the troops waited for zero on 1st July, 1916.

20. Delville Wood, 1971.

21. By Auchonvillers.

19773 PRIVATE
A. BARKER
EAST YORKSHIRE REGIMENT
1ST JULY 1916 AGE 16

BEYOND RECALL
BUT EVER IN THOUGHT
FROM THOSE WHO LOVE YOU
SO DEAR

Serre road. Here one can look up the muddy road to the hamlet of Serre, where the wrecks of some brick buildings stand in a clump of tree stumps, or half-right down a God-forgotten kind of glen, blasted by fire to the look of a moor in hell. A few rampikes of trees standing on one side of this glen give the place its name of Ten Tree Alley. Immediately to the south of the Serre road, the ground rises into one of the many big chalk spurs, which thrust from the main Hébuterne plateau towards the Ancre Valley. The spur at this point runs east and west, and the lines cross it from north and south. They go up it side by side, a hundred and fifty yards apart, with a greenish No Man's Land between them. The No Man's Land, as usual, is the only part of all this chalk spur that is not burnt, gouged, pocked, and pitted with shell fire. It is, however, enough marked by the war to be bad going. When they are well up the spur, the lines draw nearer, and at the highest point of the spur they converge in one of the terrible places of the battlefield.

For months before the battle began, it was a question here, which side should hold the highest point of the spur. Right at the top of the spur there is one patch of ground, measuring, it may be, two hundred yards each way, from which one can see a long way in every direction. From this patch, the ground droops a little towards the English side and stretches away fairly flat towards the enemy side, but one can see far either way, and to have this power of seeing, both sides fought desperately.

Until the beginning of the war, this spur of ground was corn-land, like most of the battlefield. Unfenced country roads crossed it. It was a quiet, lonely, prosperous ploughland, stretching for miles, up and down, in great sweeping rolls and folds, like our own chalk downlands. It had one feature common to all chalk countries; it was a land of smooth expanses. Before the war, all this spur was a smooth expanse, which passed in a sweep from the slope to the plateau, over this crown of summit.

To-day, the whole of the summit (which is called the Redan Ridge), for all its two hundred yards, is blown into pits and craters from twenty to fifty feet deep, and sometimes fifty yards long. These pits and ponds in rainy weather fill up with water, which pours from one pond into another, so that the hill-top is loud with the noise of the brooks. For many weeks, the armies fought for this patch of hill. It was all mined, countermined, and re-mined, and at each explosion the crater was fought for and lost and won. It cannot be said that either side won that summit till the enemy was finally beaten from all that field, for both sides conquered enough to see from. On the enemy side, a fortification of heaped earth was made; on our side, castles were built of sandbags filled with flint. These strongholds gave both sides enough observation. The works face each other across the ponds. The sandbags of the English works have now rotted, and flag about like the rags of uniform or like withered grass. The flint and chalk laid bare by their rotting look like the grey of weathered stone, so that, at a little distance, the English works look old and noble, as though they were the foundations of some castle long since fallen under Time.

To the right, that is to the southward, from these English castles there is a slope of six hundred yards into a valley or gully. The slope is not in any way remarkable or seems not to be, except that the ruin of a road, now barely to be distinguished from the field, runs across it. The opposing lines of trenches go down the slope, much as usual, with the enemy line above on a slight natural glacis. Behind this enemy line is the bulk of the spur, which is partly white from up-blown chalk, partly burnt from months of fire, and partly faintly green from recovering grass. A little to the right or south, on this bulk of spur, there are the stumps of trees and no grass at all, nothing but upturned chalk and burnt earth. On the battlefield of the Somme, these are the marks of a famous place.

The valley into which the slope descends is a broadish gentle opening in the chalk hills, with a road running at right angles to the lines of trenches at the bottom of it. As the road descends, the valley tightens in, and just where the enemy line crosses it, it becomes a narrow deep glen or gash, between high and steep banks of chalk. Well within the enemy position and fully seven hundred yards from our line, another such glen or gash runs into this glen, at right angles. At this meeting place of the glens is or was the village of Beaumont Hamel, which the enemy said could never be taken.

For the moment it need not be described ; for it was not seen by many of our men in the early stages of the battle. In fact our old line was at least five hundred yards outside it. But all our line in the valley here was opposed to the village defences, and the fighting at this point was fierce and terrible, and there are some features in the No Man's Land just outside the village which must be described. These features run parallel with our line right down to the road in the valley, and though they are not features of great tactical importance, like the patch of summit above, where the craters are, or like the windmill at Pozières, they were the last things seen by many brave Irish and Englishmen, and cannot be passed lightly by.

The features are a lane, fifty or sixty yards in front of the front trench, and a *remblai*, or lynchet, fifty or sixty yards in front of the lane.

The lane is a farmer's track leading from the road in the valley to the road on the spur. It runs almost north and south, like the lines of trenches, and is about five hundred yards long. From its start in the valley-road to a point about two hundred yards up the spur it is sunken below the level of the field on each side of it. At first the sinking is slight, but it swiftly deepens as it goes up hill. For more than a hundred yards it lies between banks twelve or fifteen feet deep. After this part the banks die down into insignificance, so that the road is nearly open. The deep part, which is like a very deep, broad, natural trench, was known to our men as the Sunken Road. The banks of this sunken part are perpendicular. Until recently, they were grown over with a scrub of dwarf beech, ash, and sturdy saplings, now mostly razed by fire. In the road itself our men built up walls of sandbags to limit the effects of enemy shell fire. From these defences steps cut in the chalk of the bank lead to the field above, where there were machine-gun pits.

The field in front of the lane (where these pits were) is a fairly smooth slope for about fifty yards. Then there is the lynchet, or *remblai*, like a steep cliff, from three to twelve feet high, hardly to be noticed from above until the traveller is upon it. Below this lynchet is a fairly smooth slope, so tilted that it slopes down to the right towards the valley road, and slopes up to the front towards the enemy line. Looking straight to the front from the Sunken Road our men saw no sudden dip down at the lynchet, but a continuous grassy field, at first flat, then slowly rising towards the enemy parapet. The line of the lynchet-top merges into the slope behind it, so that it is not seen. The enemy line thrusts out in a little salient here, so as to make the most of a little bulge of ground which was once wooded and still has stumps. The bulge is now a heap and ruin of burnt and tumbled mud and chalk. To reach it our men had to run across the flat from the Sunken Road, slide down the bank of the lynchet, and then run up the glacis to the parapet.

The Sunken Road was only held by our men as an advanced post and " jumping off " (or attacking) point. Our line lay behind it on a higher part of the spur, which does not decline gradually into the valley road, but breaks off in a steep bank cut by our soldiers into a flight of chalk steps. These steps gave to all this part of the line the name of Jacob's Ladder. From the top of Jacob's Ladder there is a good view of the valley road running down into Beaumont Hamel. To the right there is a big steep knoll of green hill bulking up to the south of the valley, and very well fenced with enemy wire. All the land to the right or south of Jacob's Ladder is this big green hill, which is very steep, irregular, and broken with banks, and so ill-adapted for trenching that we were forced to make our line further from the enemy than is usual on the front. The front trenches here are nearly five hundred yards apart.   As far as the hill-top the enemy line has a great advantage of position.   To reach it our men had to cross the open and ascend a slope which gave neither dead ground nor cover to front or flank.   Low down the hill, running parallel with the road, is a little lynchet, topped by a few old hawthorn bushes.   All this bit of the old front line was the scene of a most gallant attack by our men on the 1st of July.   Those who care may see it in the official cinematograph films of the Battle of the Somme.

Right at the top of the hill there is a dark enclosure of wood, orchard, and plantation, with several fairly well preserved red-brick buildings in it.   This is the plateau-village of Auchonvillers.   On the slopes below it, a couple of hundred yards behind Jacob's Ladder, there is a little round clump of trees.   Both village and clump make conspicuous landmarks.   The clump was once the famous English machine-gun post of the Bowery, from which our men could shoot down the valley into Beaumont Hamel.

CHAPTER IV

THE English line goes up the big green hill, in trenches and saps of reddish clay, to the plateau or tableland at the top. Right up on the top, well behind our front line and close to one of our communication trenches, there is a good big hawthorn bush, in which a magpie has built her nest. This bush, which is strangely beautiful in the spring, has given to the plateau the name of the Hawthorn Ridge.

Just where the opposing lines reach the top of the Ridge they both bend from their main north and south direction towards the south-east, and continue in that course for several miles. At the point or salient of the bending, in the old enemy position, there is a crater of a mine which the English sprang in the early morning of the 1st of July. This is the crater of the mine of Beaumont Hamel. Until recently it was supposed to be the biggest crater ever blown by one explosion. It is not the deepest : one or two others near La Boisselle are deeper, but none on the Somme field comes near it

in bigness and squalor. It is like the crater of a
volcano, vast, ragged, and irregular, about one hundred
and fifty yards long, one hundred yards across, and
twenty-five yards deep. It is crusted and scabbed with
yellowish tetter, like sulphur or the rancid fat on meat.
The inside has rather the look of meat, for it is reddish
and all streaked and scabbed with this pox and with
discoloured chalk. A lot of it trickles and oozes like
sores discharging pus, and this liquid gathers in holes
near the bottom, and is greenish and foul and has the
look of dead eyes staring upwards.

All that can be seen of it from the English line is a
disarrangement of the enemy wire and parapet. It is a
hole in the ground which cannot be seen except from
quite close at hand. At first sight, on looking into it,
it is difficult to believe that it was the work of man ;
it looks so like nature in her evil mood. It is hard to
imagine that only three years ago that hill was corn-
field, and the site of the chasm grew bread. After
that happy time, the enemy bent his line there and
made the salient a stronghold, and dug deep shelters
for his men in the walls of his trenches ; the marks of
the dugouts are still plain in the sides of the pit. Then,
on the 1st of July, when the explosion was to be a
signal for the attack, and our men waited in the trenches
for the spring, the belly of the chalk was heaved, and
chalk, clay, dugouts, gear, and enemy, went up in a

dome of blackness full of pieces, and spread aloft like a toadstool, and floated, and fell down.

From the top of the Hawthorn Ridge, our soldiers could see a great expanse of chalk downland, though the falling of the hill kept them from seeing the enemy's position. That lay on the slope of the ridge, somewhere behind the wire, quite out of sight from our lines. Looking out from our front line at this salient, our men saw the enemy wire almost as a skyline. Beyond this line, the ground dipped towards Beaumont Hamel (which was quite out of sight in the valley) and rose again sharply in the steep bulk of Beaucourt spur. Beyond this lonely spur, the hills ranked and ran, like the masses of a moor, first the high ground above Miraumont, and beyond that the high ground of the Loupart Wood, and away to the east the bulk that makes the left bank of the Ancre River. What trees there are in this moorland were not then all blasted. Even in Beaumont Hamel some of the trees were green. The trees in the Ancre River Valley made all that marshy meadow like a forest. Looking out on all this the first thought of the soldier was that here he could really see something of the enemy's ground.

It is true, that from this hill-top much land, then held by the enemy, could be seen, but very little that was vital to the enemy could be observed. His lines of supply and support ran in ravines which we could not see; his batteries lay beyond crests, his men were in hiding-places. Just below us on the lower slopes of this Hawthorn Ridge he had one vast hiding-place which gave us a great deal of trouble. This was a gully or ravine, about five hundred yards long, well within his position, running (roughly speaking) at right angles with his front line. Probably it was a steep and deep natural fold made steeper and deeper by years of cultivation. It is from thirty to forty feet deep, and about as much across at the top; it has abrupt sides, and thrusts out two forks to its southern side. These forks give it the look of a letter Y upon the maps, for which reason both the French and ourselves called the place the "Ravin en Y" or "Y Ravine." Part of the southernmost fork was slightly open to observation from our lines; the main bulk of the gully was invisible to us, except from the air.

Whenever the enemy has had a bank of any kind, at all screened from fire, he has dug into it for shelter. In the Y Ravine, which provided these great expanses of banks, he dug himself shelters of unusual strength and size. He sank shafts into the banks, tunnelled long living rooms, both above and below the gully-bottom, linked the rooms together with galleries, and cut hatchways and bolting holes to lead to the surface as well as to the gully. All this work was securely done, with baulks of seasoned wood, iron girders, and concreting. Much of it was destroyed by shell fire during the battle, but much not hit by shells is in good condition to-day even after the autumn rains and the spring thaw. The galleries which lead upwards and outwards from this underground barracks to the observation posts and machine-gun emplacements in the open air, are cunningly planned and solidly made. The posts and emplacements to which they led are now, however, (nearly all) utterly destroyed by our shell fire.

In this gully barracks, and in similar shelters cut in the chalk of the steeper banks near Beaumont Hamel, the enemy could hold ready large numbers of men to repel an attack or to make a counter-attack. They lived in these dugouts in comparative safety and in moderate comfort. When our attacks came during the early months of the battle, they were able to pass rapidly and safely by these underground galleries from one part of the position to another, bringing their machine guns with them. However, the Ravine was presently taken and the galleries and underground shelters were cleared. In one underground room in that barracks, nearly fifty of the enemy were found lying dead in their bunks, all unwounded, and as though asleep. They had been killed by the concussion of the air following on the burst of a big shell at the entrance.

One other thing may be mentioned about this Hawthorn Ridge. It runs parallel with the next spur (the Beaucourt spur) immediately to the north of it, then in the enemy's hands. Just over the crest of this spur, out of sight from our lines, is a country road, well banked and screened, leading from Beaucourt to Serre. This road was known by our men as Artillery Lane, because it was used as a battery position by the enemy. The wrecks of several of his guns lie in the mud there still. From the crest in front of this road there is a view to the westward, so wonderful that those who see it realize at once that the enemy position on the Ridge, which, at a first glance, seems badly sited for observation, is, really, well placed. From this crest, the Ridge-top, all our old front line, and nearly all the No Man's Land upon it, is exposed, and plainly to be seen. On a reasonably clear day, no man could leave our old line unseen from this crest. No artillery officer, correcting the fire of a battery, could ask for a better place from which to watch the bursts of his shells. This crest, in front of the lane of enemy guns, made it possible for the enemy batteries to drop shells upon our front line trenches before all the men were out of them at the instant of the great attack.

The old English line runs along the Hawthorn Ridge-top for some hundreds of yards, and then crosses a dip or valley, which is the broad, fan-shaped, southern end of a fork of Y Ravine. A road runs, or ran, down this dip into the Y Ravine. It is not now recognizable as a road, but the steep banks at each side of it, and some bluish metalling in the shell holes, show that one once ran there. These banks are covered with hawthorn bushes. A *remblai*, also topped with hawthorn, lies a little to the north of this road.

From this lynchet, looking down the valley into the Y Ravine, the enemy position s saddle-shaped, low in the middle, where the Y Ravine narrows, and rising to right and left to a good height. Chalk hills from their form often seem higher than they really are, especially in any kind of haze. Often they have mystery and nearly always beauty. For some reason, the lumping rolls of chalk hill rising up on each side of this valley have a menace and a horror about them. One sees little of the enemy position from the English line. It is now nothing but a track of black wire in front of some burnt and battered heapings of the ground, upon which the grass and the flowers have only now begun to push. At the beginning of the battle it must have been greener and fresher, for then the fire of hell had not come upon it; but even then, even in the summer day, that dent in the chalk leading to the Y Ravine must have seemed a threatening and forbidding place.

Our line goes along the top of the ridge here, at a

good distance from the enemy line. It is dug on the brow of the plateau in reddish earth on the top of chalk. It is now much as our men left it for the last time. The trench-ladders by which they left it are still in place in the bays of the trenches. All the outer, or jumping-off, trenches, are much destroyed by enemy shell fire, which was very heavy here from both sides of the Ancre River. A quarter of a mile to the south-east of the Y Ravine the line comes within sight of the great gap which cuts the battlefield in two. This gap is the valley of the Ancre River, which runs here beneath great spurs of chalk, as the Thames runs at Goring and Pangbourne. On the lonely hill, where this first comes plainly into view, as one travels south along the line, there used to be two bodies of English soldiers, buried once, and then unburied by the rain. They lay in the No Man's Land, outside the English wire, in what was then one of the loneliest places in the field. The ruin of war lay all round them.

There are many English graves (marked, then, hurriedly, by the man's rifle thrust into the ground) in that piece of the line. On a windy day, these rifles shook in the wind as the bayonets bent to the blast. The field testaments of both men lay open beside them in the mud. The rain and the mud together had nearly destroyed the little books, but in each case it was possible to read one text. In both cases, the text which remained, read with a strange irony. The one book, beside a splendid youth, cut off in his promise, was open at a text which ran, "And Moses was learned in all the wisdom of the Egyptians and mighty in word and in deed." The other book, beside one who had been killed in an attack which did not succeed at the moment, but which led to the falling back of the enemy nation from many miles of conquered ground, read even more strangely. It was open at the eighty-ninth Psalm, and the only legible words were, "Thou hast broken down all his hedges; thou hast brought his strong holds to ruin."

From the hill-top where these graves are the lines droop down towards the second of the four roads, which runs here in the Ancre valley parallel with the river and the railway. The slope is steep and the ground broken with shallow gullies and lynchets. Well down towards the river, just above the road, a flattish piece of land leads to a ravine with steep and high banks. This flattish land, well within the enemy line, was the scene of very desperate fighting on the 1st of July.

Looking at the enemy line in front of our own line here, one sees little but a gentle crest, protected by wire, in front of another gentle crest, also wired, with other gentle crests beyond and to the left. To the right there is a blur of gentle crests behind tree-tops.

It is plain from a glance that gullies run irregularly
into the spurs here, and make the defence easy.   All
through the fighting here, it happened too often that
the taking of one crest only meant that the winners
were taken in flank by machine guns in the crest beyond,
and (in this bit of the line) by other guns on the other
side of the river.

Well to the back of the English line here, on the top
of the plateau, level with Auchonvillers, some trees
stand upon the skyline, with the tower of a church,
battered, but not destroyed, like the banner of some
dauntless one, a little to the west of the wood.   The
wood shows marks of shelling, but nothing like the
marks on the woods attacked by our own men.   There
are signs of houses among the trees, and the line of a
big wood to the east of them.

This church and the buildings near it are parts of
Mesnil village, most of which lies out of sight on the
further side of the crest.   They are conspicuous landmarks, and can be made out from many parts of the
field.   The chalk scarp on which they stand is by much
the most beautiful thing on the battlefield, and the
sight of Mesnil church tower on the top of it is most
pleasant.   That little banner stood all through the war,
and not all the guns of the enemy could bring it down.
Many men in the field near Mesnil, enduring the mud
of the thaw, and the lice, wet, and squalor of dugouts

near the front, were cheered by that church tower.
" For all their bloody talk the bastards couldn't bring
it down."

The hill with the lines upon it slopes steeply down
to the valley of the Ancre. Just where the lines come
to the valley, the ground drops abruptly, in a cliff or
steep bank, twenty-five feet high, to the road.

Our line on this slope covers the village of Hamel,
which lies just behind the line, along the road and on
the hill-slopes above it. The church and churchyard
of Hamel, both utterly ruined, lie well up the hill in
such a position that they made good posts from which
our snipers could shoot across the river at men in the
Schwaben Redoubt. Crocuses, snowdrops, and a purple
flower once planted on the graves of the churchyard,
but now escaped into the field, blossomed here in
this wintry spring, long before any other plant on
the battlefield was in bud.

Hamel in peace time may have contained forty houses,
some shatters of which still stand. There are a few
red-brick walls, some frames of wood from which the
plaster has been blown, some gardens gone wild, fruit
trees unpruned and more or less ragged from fire, and
an air of desecration and desertion. In some of the
ruins there are signs of use. The lower windows are
filled with sandbags, the lower stories are strengthened
with girders and baulks. From the main road in the

valley, a country track or road, muddy even for the Somme, leads up the hill, through the heart of the village, past the church, towards our old line and Auchonvillers.

Not much can be seen from the valley road in Hamel, for it is only a few feet above the level of the river-bed, which is well grown with timber not yet completely destroyed. The general view to the eastward from this low-lying road is that of a lake, five hundred yards across, in some wild land not yet settled. The lake is shallow, blind with reeds, vivid with water-grass, and lively with moor-fowl. The trees grow out of the water, or lie in it, just as they fell when they were shot. On the whole, the trees just here, though chipped and knocked about, have not suffered badly; they have the look of trees, and are leafy in summer. Beyond the trees, on the other side of the marsh, is the steep and high eastern bank of the Ancre, on which a battered wood, called Thiepval Wood, stands like an army of black and haggard rampikes. But for this stricken wood, the eastern bank of the Ancre is a gentle, sloping hill, bare of trees. On the top of this hill is the famous Schwaben Redoubt.

The Ancre River and the marshy valley through which it runs are crossed by several causeways. One most famous causeway crosses just in front of Hamel on the line of the old Mill Road. The Mill from which it takes its name lies to the left of the causeway on a sort of green island. The wheel, which is not destroyed, still shows among the ruins. The enemy had a dressing station there at one time.

The marshy valley of the Ancre splits up the river here into several channels besides the mill stream. The channels are swift and deep, full of exquisitely clear water just out of the chalk. The marsh is rather blind with snags cut off by shells. For some years past the moor-fowl in the marsh have been little molested. They are very numerous here ; their cries make the place lonely and romantic.

When one stands on this causeway over the Ancre one is almost at the middle point of the battlefield, for the river cuts the field in two. Roughly speaking, the ground to the west of the river was the scene of continuous fighting, the ground to the east of the river the scene of our advance. At the eastern end of the causeway the Old Mill Road rises towards the Schwaben Redoubt.

CHAPTER V

ALL the way up the hill the road is steep, rather deep, and bad. It is worn into the chalk and shows up very white in sunny weather. Before the battle it lay about midway between the lines, but it was always patrolled at night by our men. The ground on both sides of it is almost more killed and awful than anywhere in the field. On the English or south side of it, distant from one hundred to two hundred yards, is the shattered wood, burnt, dead, and desolate. On the enemy side, at about the same distance, is the usual black enemy wire, much tossed and bunched by our shells, covering a tossed and tumbled chalky and filthy parapet. Our own old line is an array of rotted sandbags, filled with chalk-flint, covering the burnt wood. One need only look at the ground to know that the fighting here was very grim, and to the death. Near the road and up the slope to the enemy the ground is littered with relics of our charges, mouldy packs, old shattered scabbards, rifles, bayonets, helmets curled, torn, rolled, and starred, clips of cartridges, and very many graves. Many of the graves are marked with strips of wood torn from packing cases, with pencilled inscriptions, " An unknown British Hero "; " In loving memory of Pte. ———"; " Two unknown British heroes "; " An unknown British soldier "; "A dead Fritz." That gentle slope to the Schwaben is covered with such things.

Passing these things, by some lane through the wire and clambering over the heaps of earth which were once the parapet, one enters the Schwaben, where so much life was spent. As in so many places on this old battlefield, the first thought is: " Why, they were in an eyrie here ; our fellows had no chance at all." There is no wonder, then, that the approach is strewn with graves. The line stands at the top of a smooth, open slope, commanding our old position and the Ancre Valley. There is no cover of any kind upon the slope except the rims of the shell-holes, which make rings of mud among the grass. Just outside the highest point of the front line there is a little clump of our graves. Just inside there is a still unshattered concrete fortlet, built for the machine gun by which those men were killed.

All along that front trench of the Schwaben, lying on the parapet, half buried in the mud, are the belts of machine guns, still full of cartridges. There were many machine guns on that earthen wall last year. When our men scrambled over the tumbled chalky line of old sandbags, so plain just down the hill, and came into view on the slope, running and stumbling in the hour of the attack, the machine gunners in the fortress felt indeed that they were in an eyrie, and that our fellows had no chance at all.

For the moment one thinks this, as the enemy gunners must have thought it; then, looking up the hill at the inner works of the great fort, the thought comes that it was not so happy a fate to have to hold this eyrie. Sometimes, in winter storms, the Atlantic is heaved aloft and tossed and tumbled under an evil heaven till all its wilderness is hideous. This hill-top is exactly as though some such welter of water had suddenly become mud. It is all heaped and tossed and tumbled as though the earth there had been a cross-sea. In one place some great earth wave of a trench has been bitten into and beaten back and turned blind into an eddy by great pits and chasms and running heaps. Then in another place, where the crown of the work once reared itself aloft over the hill, the heaps of mud are all blurred and pounded together, so that there is no design, no trace, no visible plan of any fortress, only a mess of mud bedevilled and bewildered. All this mess of heaps and hillocks is strung and filthied over with broken bodies and ruined gear. There is nothing whole, nor alive, nor clean, in all its extent; it is a place of ruin and death, blown and blasted out of any likeness to any work of man, and so smashed that there is no shelter on it, save for the one machine gunner in his box. On all that desolate hill our fire fell like rain for days and nights and weeks, till the watchers in our line could see no hill at all, but a great, vague, wreathing devil of darkness in which little sudden fires winked and glimmered and disappeared.

Once in a lull of the firing a woman appeared upon the enemy parapet and started to walk along it. Our men held their fire and watched her. She walked steadily along the whole front of the Schwaben and then jumped down into her trench. Many thought at the time that she was a man masquerading for a bet, but long afterwards, when our men took the Schwaben, they found her lying in the ruins dead. They buried her there, up on the top of the hill. God alone knows who she was and what she was doing there.

Looking back across the Ancre from the Schwaben the hill of the right bank of the river is clear from the woods near Mesnil to Beaucourt. All along that graceful chalk hill our communication trenches thrust up like long white mole-runs, or like the comb of rollers on a reef. At right angles to these long white lines are black streaks which mark the enemy's successive front lines. The later ones are visibly more ragged than those near our old line.

There are few more lonely places than that scene of old battles. One may stand on the Schwaben for many days together and look west over the moor, or east over the wilderness, without seeing any sign of human life, save perhaps some solitary guarding a dump of stores.

The hill on which the Schwaben is built is like a great thumb laid down beside the Ancre River. There is a little valley on its eastern side exactly like the space between a great thumb and a great forefinger. It is called Crucifix Valley, from an iron Calvary that stood in it in the early days of the war. It must once have been a lovely and romantic glen, strangely beautiful throughout. Even now its lower reach between a steep bank of scrub and Thiepval Wood is as lovely as a place can be after the passing of a cyclone. Its upper reach, which makes the eastern boundary of the Schwaben, is as ghastly a scene of smash as the world can show. It is nothing but a collection of irregular pools dug by big shells during months of battle. The pools are long enough and deep enough to dive into, and full to overflowing with filthy water. Sometimes the pressure of the water bursts the mud banks of one of these pools and a rush of water comes, and the pools below it overflow, and a noise of water rises in that solitude which is like the mud and water of the beginning of the world before any green thing appeared.

Our line runs across this Crucifix Valley in a strong sandbag barricade. The enemy line crosses it higher up in a continuation of the front line of the Schwaben. As soon as the lines are across the valley they turn sharply to the south at an important point.

The Schwaben spur is like a thumb; Crucifix Valley is like the space between a thumb and a forefinger. Just to the east of Crucifix Valley a second spur thrusts away down to the south like a forefinger. It is a long sloping spur, wooded at the lower end. It is known on the maps as Thiepval Hill or the Leipzig Salient. When the lines turn to the south after crossing Crucifix Valley they run along the side of this hill and pass out of sight round the end. The lines are quite regular and distinct. From the top of the Schwaben it looks as though the side of the hill were fenced into a neat green track or racecourse. This track is the No Man's Land, which lies like a broad green regular stripe between brown expanses along the hillside. All this hill was of the greatest importance to the enemy. It was as strong an eyrie as the Schwaben; it turned and made very dangerous our works in front of Hamel; and it was the key to a covered way to the plateau from which all these spurs thrust southward.

It is a bolder, more regular spur than the others which thrust from this plateau. The top slopes so slightly as to be almost level, the two flanks are rather steep.

Right at the top of it, just where it springs from the plateau, much where the knuckle of the imagined hand would be, and perhaps five hundred yards east from our old sandbag barricade in Crucifix Valley, there is a redness in the battered earth and upon the chalk of the road. The redness is patchy over a good big stretch of this part of the spur, but it is all within the enemy lines and well above our own. Where the shattered hillside slopes towards our lines there are many remnants of trees, some of them fruit trees arranged in a kind of order behind the burnt relics of a hedge, others dotted about at random. All are burnt, blasted, and killed. One need only glance at the hill on which they stand to see that it has been more burnt and shell-smitten than most parts of the lines. It is as though the fight here had been more than to the death, to beyond death, to the bones and skeleton of the corpse which was yet unkillable. This is the site of the little hill village of Thiepval, which once stood at a cross-roads here among apple orchards and the trees of a park. It had a church, just at the junction of the roads, and a fine seigneurial château, in a garden, beside the church; otherwise it was a little lonely mean place, built of brick and plaster on a great lonely heap of chalk downland. It had no importance and no history before the war, except that a Seigneur of Thiepval is mentioned as having once attended a meeting at Amiens. It was of great military importance at the time of the Battle of the Somme. In the old days it may have had a beauty of position.

It is worth while to clamber up to Thiepval from our lines. The road runs through the site of the village in a deep cutting, which may once have been lovely. The road is reddish with the smashed bricks of the village. Here and there in the mud are perhaps three courses of brick where a house once stood, or some hideous hole bricked at the bottom for the vault of a cellar. Blasted, dead, pitted stumps of trees, with their bark in rags, grow here and there in a collection of vast holes, ten feet deep and fifteen feet across, with filthy water in them. There is nothing left of the church; a big reddish mound of brick, that seems mainly powder round a core of cement, still marks where the château stood. The château garden, the round village pond, the pine-tree which was once a landmark there, are all blown out of recognition.

The mud of the Somme, which will be remembered by our soldiers long after they have forgotten the shelling, was worse at Thiepval than elsewhere, or, at least, could not have been worse elsewhere. The road through Thiepval was a bog, the village was a quagmire. Near the château there were bits where one sank to the knee. In the great battle for Thiepval, on the 26th of last September, one of our Tanks charged an enemy

trench here. It plunged and stuck fast and remained
in the mud, like a great animal stricken dead in its
spring. It was one of the sights of Thiepval during the
winter, for it looked most splendid; afterwards, it was
salved and went to fight again.

From this part of Thiepval one can look along the
top of the Leipzig Spur, which begins here and thrusts
to the south for a thousand yards.

There are two big enemy works on the Leipzig Spur :
one, well to the south of the village, is (or was, for it is
all blown out of shape) a six-angled star-shaped redoubt
called the Wonder Work; the other, still further to the
south, about a big, disused, and very evil-looking quarry,
towards the end of the spur, is, or was, called the
Leipzig Salient, or, by some people, the Hohenzollern,
from the Hohenzollern Trench, which ran straight across
the spur about halfway down the salient.

In these two fortresses the enemy had two strong,
evil eyries, high above us. They look down upon our
line, which runs along the side of the hill below them.
Though, in the end, our guns blasted the enemy off the
hill, our line along that slope was a costly one to hold,
since fire upon it could be observed and directed from
so many points—from the rear (above Hamel), from the
left flank (on the Schwaben and near Thiepval), and
from the hill itself. The hill is all skinned and scarred,
and the trace of the great works can no longer be

followed. At the top of the hill, in the middle of a
filthy big pool, is a ruined enemy trench-mortar, sitting
up like a swollen toad.

At the end of the spur the lines curve round to the
east to shut in the hill. A grass-grown road crosses
the lines here, goes up to the hill-top, and then along
it. The slopes at this end of the hill are gentle, and
from low down, where our lines are, it is a pleasant and
graceful brae, where the larks never cease to sing and
where you may always put up partridges and sometimes
even a hare. It is a deserted hill at this time, but for
the wild things. The No Man's Land is littered with
the relics of a charge ; for many brave Dorsetshire and
Wiltshire men died in the rush up that slope. On the
highest point of the enemy parapet, at the end of the
hill, is a lonely white cross, which stands out like a
banner planted by a conqueror. It marks the grave of
an officer of the Wilts, who was killed there, among the
ruin, in the July attack.

Below the lines, where the ground droops away
towards the river, the oddly shaped, deeply valleyed
Wood of Authuille begins. It makes a sort of socket
of woodland so curved as to take the end of the spur.

It is a romantic and very lovely wood, pleasant with
the noise of water and not badly damaged by the
fighting. The trees are alive and leafy, the shrubs are
pushing, and the spring flowers, wood anemones,

violets, and the oxlip (which in this country takes the place of the primrose and the cowslip) flower beautifully among the shell-holes, rags, and old tins of war, But at the north-eastern end it runs out in a straggling spinney along the Leipzig's east flank, and this horn of wood is almost as badly shattered as if the shell fire upon it had been English. Here the enemy, fearing for his salient, kept up a terrible barrage. The trees are burnt, ragged, unbarked, topped, and cut off short, the trenches are blown in and jumbled, and the ground blasted and gouged.

Standing in the old English front line just to the north of Authuille Wood, one sees the usual slow gradual grassy rise to the dark enemy wire. Mesnil stands out among its trees to the left; to the right is this shattered stretch of wood, with a valley beyond it, and a rather big, steep, green hill topped by a few trees beyond the valley. The jut of the Leipzig shuts out the view to the flanks, so that one can see little more than this.

The Leipzig, itself, like the Schwaben, is a hawk's nest or eyrie. Up there one can look down by Authuille Wood to Albert church and chimneys, the uplands of the Somme, the Amiens road, down which the enemy marched in triumph and afterwards retreated in a hurry, and the fair fields that were to have been the booty of this war. Away to the left of this is the wooded clump of Bécourt, and, beyond it, One Tree Hill with its forlorn mound, like the burial place of a King. On the right flank is the Ancre Valley, with the English position round Hamel like an open book under the eye; on the left flank is the rather big, steep, green hill, topped by a few trees, before mentioned. These trees grow in and about what was once the village of Ovillers-la-Boisselle. The hill does not seem to have a name; it may be called here Middle Finger Hill or Ovillers Hill.

Like the Schwaben and the Leipzig Hills this hill thrusts out from the knuckle of the big chalk plateau to the north of it like the finger of a hand, in this case the middle finger. It is longer and less regularly defined than the Leipzig Hill; because instead of ending, it merges into other hills not quite so high. The valley which parts it from the Leipzig is steeply sided, with the banks of great lynchets. The lines cross the valley obliquely and run north and south along the flank of this hill, keeping their old relative positions, the enemy line well above our own, so that the approach to it is up a glacis.

As one climbs up along our old line here, the great flank of Ovillers Hill is before one in a noble, bare sweep of grass, running up to the enemy line. Something in the make of this hill, in its shape, or in the way it catches the light, gives it a strangeness which other parts of the battlefield have not.   The rise between the lines of the trenches is fully two hundred yards across, perhaps more.   Nearly all over it, in no sort of order, now singly, now in twos or threes, just as the men fell, are the crosses of the graves of the men who were killed in the attack there.   Here and there among the little crosses is one bigger than the rest, to some man specially loved or to the men of some battalion. It is difficult to stand in the old English line from which those men started without the feeling that the crosses are the men alive, still going forward, as they went in the July morning a year ago.

Just within the enemy line, three-quarters ot the way up the hill, there is a sort of small flat field about fifty yards across where the enemy lost very heavily.   They must have gathered there for some rush and then been caught by our guns.

At the top of the hill the lines curve to the south-east, drawing closer together.   The crest of the hill, such as it is, was not bitterly disputed here, for we could see all that we wished to see of the hill from the eastern flank.   Our line passes over the spur slightly below it, the enemy line takes in as much of it as the enemy needed.   From it, he has a fair view of Albert town and of the country to the east and west of it, the wooded hill of Bécourt, and the hill above Fricourt. From our line, we see his line and a few tree-tops.

From the eastern flank of the hill, our line gives a glimpse of the site of the village of Ovillers-la-Boisselle, once one of the strong places of the enemy, and now a few heaps of bricks, and one spike of burnt ruin where the church stood.

Like most Picardy villages, Ovillers was compactly built of red brick along a country road, with trees and orchards surrounding it.   It had a lofty and pretentious brick church of a modern type. Below and beyond it to the east is a long and not very broad valley which lies between the eastern flank of Ovillers Hill and the next spur. It is called Mash Valley on the maps. The lines go down Ovillers Hill into this valley and then across it.

Right at the upper end of this valley, rather more than a mile away, yet plainly visible from our lines near Ovillers, at the time of the beginning of the battle, were a few red-brick ruins in an irregular row across the valley-head. A clump of small fir and cypress trees stood up dark on the hill at the western end of this row, and behind the trees was a line of green hill topped with the ruins of a windmill. The ruins, now gone, were the end of Pozières village, the dark trees grew in Pozières cemetery, and the mill was the famous windmill of Pozières, which marked the crest that was one of the prizes of the battle. All these things were then clearly to be seen, though in the distance.

The main hollow of the valley is not remarkable except

that it is crossed by enormous trenches and very steeply hedged by a hill on its eastern flank. This eastern hill which has such a steep side is a spur or finger of chalk thrusting southward from Pozières, like the ring-finger of the imagined hand. Mash Valley curves round its finger-tip, and just at the spring of the curve the third of the four Albert roads crosses it, and goes up the spur towards Pozières and Bapaume. The line of the road, which is rather banked up, so as to be a raised way, like so many Roman roads, can be plainly seen, going along the spur, almost to Pozières. In many places, it makes the eastern skyline to observers down in the valley.

Behind our front line in this Mash Valley is the pleasant green Usna Hill, which runs across the hollow and shuts it in to the south. From this hill, seamed right across with our reserve and support trenches, one can look down at the enemy position, which crosses Mash Valley in six great lines all very deep, strong, and dug into for underground shelter.

CHAPTER VI

STANDING in Mash Valley, at the foot of Ring Finger Spur, just where the Roman Road starts its long rise to Pozières, one sees a lesser road forking off to the right, towards a village called Contalmaison, a couple of miles away. The fork of the road marks where our old front line ran. The trenches are filled in at this point now, so that the roads may be used, but the place was once an exceedingly hot corner. In the old days, all the space between the two roads at the fork was filled with the village or hamlet of La Boisselle, which, though a tiny place, had once a church and perhaps a hundred inhabitants. The enemy fortified the village till it was an exceedingly strong place. We held a part of the village cemetery. Some of the broken crosses of the graves still show among the chalk here.

To the left of the Roman Road, only a stone's-throw from this ruined graveyard, a part of our line is built up with now rotting sandbags full of chalk, so that it looks like a mound of grey rocks. Opposite the mound,

perhaps a hundred yards up the hill, is another, much
bigger, irregular mound, of chalk that has become dirty,
with some relics of battered black wire at its base.
The space between the two mounds is now green with
grass, though pitted with shell-holes, and marked in
many places with the crosses of graves. The space is
the old No Man's Land, and the graves are of men who
started to charge across that field on the 1st of July.
The big grey mound is the outer wall or casting of a
mine thirty yards deep in the chalk and a hundred
yards across, which we sprang under the enemy line
there on that summer morning, just before our men
went over.

La Boisselle, after being battered by us in our attack,
was destroyed by enemy fire after we had taken it, and
then cleared by our men who wished to use the roads.
It offers no sight of any interest ; but just outside it,
between the old lines, there is a stretch of spur, useful
for observation, for which both sides fought bitterly.
For about 200 yards, the No Man's Land is a succes-
sion of pits in the chalk where mines have been sprung.
Chalk, wire, stakes, friends, and enemies seem here to
have been all blown to powder.

The lines cross this debated bit, and go across a small,
ill-defined bulk of chalk, known as Chapes Spur, on the
top of which there is a vast heap of dazzlingly white
chalk, so bright that it is painful to look at.   Beyond it

is the pit of a mine, evenly and cleanly blown, thirty-five yards deep, and more than a hundred yards across, in the pure chalk of the upland, as white as cherry blossom. This is the finest, though not the biggest, mine in the battlefield. It was the work of many months, for the shafts by which it was approached began more than a quarter of a mile away. It was sprung on the 1st of July as a signal for the attack. Quite close to it are the graves of an officer and a sergeant, both English, who were killed in the attack a few minutes after that chasm in the chalk had opened. The sergeant was killed while trying to save his officer.

The lines bend down south-eastward from Chapes Spur, and cross a long, curving, shallow valley, known as Sausage Valley, famous, later in the battle, as an assembly place for men going up against Pozières. Here the men in our line could see nothing but chalk slope to right, left, or front, except the last tree of La Boisselle, rising gaunt and black above the line of the hill. Just behind them, however, at the foot of the Sausage Valley they had a pleasant wooded hill, the hill of Bécourt, which was for nearly two years within a mile of the front line, yet remained a green and leafy hill, covered with living trees, among which the château of Bécourt remained a habitable house.

The lines slant in a south-easterly direction across the Sausage Valley; they mount the spur to the east of it, and proceed, in the same direction, across a bare field, like the top of a slightly tilted table, in the long slope down to Fricourt. Here, the men in our front lines could see rather more from their position. In front of them was a smooth space of grass slightly rising to the enemy lines two hundred yards away. Behind the enemy lines is a grassy space, and behind this, there shows what seems to be a gully or ravine, beyond which the high ground of another spur rises, much as the citadel of an old encampment rises out of its walled ditch. This high ground of this other spur is not more than a few feet above the ground near it, but it is higher; it commands it. All the high ground is wooded. To the southern or lower end of it the trees are occasional and much broken by fire. To the northern or upper end they grow in a kind of wood though all are much destroyed. Right up to the wood, all the high ground bears traces of building; there are little tumbles of bricks and something of the colour of brick all over the pilled, poxed, and blasted heap that is so like an old citadel. The ravine in front of it is the gully between the two spurs; it shelters the sunken road to Contalmaison; the heap is Fricourt village, and the woodland to the north is Fricourt Wood. A glance is enough to show that it is a strong position.

To the left of Fricourt, the spur rises slowly into a skyline. To the right the lines droop down the spur to a valley, across a brook and a road in the valley, and up a big bare humping chalk hill placed at right angles to the spur on which Fricourt stands.

The spur on which Fricourt stands and the spur down which the lines run both end at the valley in a steep drop.　Just above the steep fall our men fought very hard to push back the enemy a little towards Fricourt, so that he might not see the lower part of the valley, or be able to enfilade our lines on the other side of it.　For about three hundred yards here the space between the lines is filled with the craters of mines exploded under the enemy's front line.　In some cases, we seized and held the craters; in others the craters were untenable by either side.　Under one of those held by us it was found that the enemy had sunk a big counter-mine, which was excavated and ready for charging at the time of the beginning of the battle, when Fricourt fell.　This part of the line is more thickly coated with earth than most of the chalk hills of the battlefield.　The craters lie in a blown and dug up wilderness of heaps of reddish earth, pocked with shell-holes, and tumbled with wire.　The enemy lines are much broken and ruined, their parapets thrown down, the mouths of their dugouts blown in, and their pride abased.

The Fricourt position was one of the boasts of the enemy on this front.　Other places on the line, such as the Leipzig, the Schwaben, and the trenches near Hamel, were strong, because they could be supported by works behind them or on their flanks. Fricourt was strong in itself, like Gommecourt. It was perhaps the only place in the field of which it could be said that it was as strong as Gommecourt. As at Gommecourt, it had a good natural glacis up to the front line, which was deep, strong, and well wired. Behind the front line was a wired second line, and behind that, the rising spur on which the village stood, commanding both with machine-gun emplacements.

Fricourt was not captured by storm, but swiftly isolated and forced to surrender. It held out not quite two days. It was the first first-rate fortress taken by our men from the enemy in this engagement. In the ruins, they saw for the first time the work which the enemy puts into his main defences, and the skill and craft with which he provides for his comfort. For some weeks, the underground arrangements of Fricourt, the stairs with wired treads, the bolting holes, the air and escape shafts, the living rooms with electric light, the panelled walls, covered with cretonnes of the smartest Berlin patterns, the neat bunks and the signs of female visitors, were written of in the press, so that some may think that Fricourt was better fitted than other places on the line. It is not so. The work at Fricourt was well done, but it was no better than that at other places, where a village with cellars in it had to be converted into a fortress. Our men took Fricourt at the beginning of the battle, in a fair state of preservation. Such work was then new to our men, and this good example was made much of.

In the valley below the village, in great, deep, and powerfully revetted works, the enemy had built himself gun emplacements, so weighted with timber balks that they collapsed soon after his men ceased to attend them. The line of these great works ran (as so many of his important lines have run) at the foot of a steep bank or lynchet, so that at a little distance the parapet of the work merged into the bank behind it and was almost invisible. This line of guns ran about east and west across the neck of the Fricourt Salient, which thrust still further south, across the little valley and up the hill on the other side.

CHAPTER VII

OUR old line crosses the valley just to the east of the Fricourt Station on the little railway which once ran in the valley past Fricourt and Mametz to Montauban. It then crossed the fourth of the roads from Albert, at Fricourt cemetery, which is a small, raised forlorn garden of broken tombs at a cross-roads, under the hill facing Fricourt. Here our line began to go diagonally up the lower slopes of the hill. The enemy line climbed it further to the east, round the bulging snout of the hill, at a steep and difficult point above the bank of a sunken road. Towards the top of the hill the lines converged.

All the way of the hill, the enemy had the stronger position. It was above us almost invisible and unguessable, except from the air, at the top of a steep climb up a clay bank, which in wet weather makes bad going even for the Somme; and though the lie of the ground made it impossible for him to see much of our position, it was impossible for us to see anything of his or to assault him. The hill is a big steep chalk hill, with contours so laid upon it that not much of it can be seen from below. By looking to the left from our trenches on its western lower slopes one can see nothing of Fricourt, for the bulge of the hill's snout covers it. One has a fair view of the old English line on the smoothish big slope between Fricourt and Bécourt, but nothing of the enemy stronghold. One might have lived in those trenches for nearly two years without seeing any enemy except the rain and mud and lice.

Up at the top of the hill, there is an immense prospect over the eastern half of the battlefield, and here, where the lines converge, it was most necessary for us to have the crest and for the enemy to keep us off it. The highest ground is well forward, on the snout, and this point was the only part of the hill which the enemy strove to keep. His line goes up the hill to the highest point, cuts off the highest point, and at once turns eastward, so that his position on the hill is just the northern slope and a narrow line of crest. It is as though an army holding Fleet Street against an army on the Embankment and in Cheapside should have seized Ludgate Hill to the top of the steps of St. Paul's and left the body of the cathedral to its opponent. The lines securing this important salient are of immense strength and intricacy, with many great avenues of approach. The front line is double across the greater part of the crest, and behind it is a very deep, strong, trebly wired support line which is double at important points.

Our old front line runs almost straight across the crest parallel with the enemy front line, and distant from it from forty to one hundred and fifty yards. The crest or highest ground is on both flanks of the hill-top close to the enemy line. Between the lines at both these points are the signs of a struggle which raged for weeks and months for the possession of those lumps of hill, each, perhaps, two hundred yards long, by fifty broad, by five high. Those fifteen feet of height were bartered for with more than their own weight of sweat and blood ; the hill can never lose the marks of the struggle.

In those two patches of the hill the space between the lines is a quarry of confluent craters, twenty or thirty yards deep, blown into and under each other till the top of the hill is split apart. No man can now tell which of all these mines were sunk by our men. The quarry runs irregularly in heaps and hollows of chalk and red earth mingled like flesh and blood. On our side of the pits the marks of our occupation are plain. There in several places, as at La Boisselle and on the Beaucourt spur, our men have built up the parapet of our old front line by thousands of sandbags till it is a hill-top or cairn from which they could see beyond.

The sandbags have rotted and the chalk and flints within have fallen partly through the rags, and Nature has already begun to change those heaps to her own colours, but they will be there for ever as the mark of our race. Such monuments must be as lasting as Stonehenge. Neither the mines nor the guns of the enemy could destroy them. From among them our soldiers peered through the smoke of burning and explosions at the promised land which the battle made ours.

From those heaps there is a wide view over that part of the field. To the left one sees Albert, the wooded clump of Bécourt, and a high green spur which hides the Sausage Valley. To the front this green spur runs to the higher ground from which the Fricourt spur thrusts. On this higher ground, behind Fricourt and its wood, is a much bigger, thicker, and better grown wood, about a mile and a half away; this is the wood of Mametz. Some short distance to the left of this wood, very plainly visible on the high, rather bare hill, is a clump of pollarded trees near a few heaps of red brick. The trees were once the shade-giving trees about the market-place of Contalmaison, a hamlet at a cross-roads at this point. Behind these ruins the sky-line is a kind of ridge which runs in a straight line, broken in one place by a few shatters of trees. These trees are the remains of the wood which once grew outside the village of Pozières. The ridge is the Albert-Bapaume Road, here passing over the highest ground on its path.

Turning from these distant places and looking to the right, one sees, just below, twelve hundred yards to the east of Fricourt, across the valley at the foot of this hill of the salient, the end of an irregular spur, on which are the shattered bricks of the village of Mametz before mentioned.

To the north of Mametz the ground rises. From the eyrie of the salient one can look over it and away to the north to big rolling chalk land, most of it wooded. Mametz Wood is a dark expanse to the front; to the right of it are other woods, Bazentin Woods, Big and Little, and beyond them, rather to the right and only just visible as a few sticks upon the skyline, are two other woods, High Wood, like a ghost in the distance, and the famous and terrible Wood of Delville. High Wood is nearly five miles away and a little out of the picture. The other wooded heights are about three miles away. All that line of high ground marked by woods was the enemy second line, which with a few slight exceptions was our front line before the end of the third week of the battle.

From this hill-top of the salient the lines run down the north-eastern snout of the hill and back across the valley, so as to shut in Mametz. Then they run eastward for a couple of miles, up to and across a plateau in front of the hamlet of Carnoy, which was just within our line. From our line, in this bare and hideous field, little could be seen but the slope up to the enemy line. At one point, where the road or lane from Carnoy to Montauban crossed the enemy line, there was a struggle for the power to see, and as a result of the struggle mines and counter-mines were sprung here till the space between the lines is now a chaos of pits and chasms full of water. The country here is an expanse of smoothish tilted slopes, big, empty, and lonely, and crossed (at about the middle point) by a strange narrow gut or gully, up which the railway once ran to Montauban. No doubt there are places in the English chalk counties which resemble this sweep of country, but I know of none so bare or so featureless. The ground is of the reddish earth which makes such bad mud. The slopes are big and gradual, either up or down. Little breaks the monotony of the expanse except a few copses or sites of copses; the eye is always turning to the distance.

In front, more than half a mile away, the ground reaches its highest point in the ridge or bank which marks the road to Montauban. The big gradual sweep up is only broken by lines of trenches and by mud heaped up from the road. Some of the trees which once made Montauban pleasant and shady still stand over the little heaps of brick and solitary iron gate which show where the village used to stand. Rather to the right of this, and nearer to our lines, are some irregular red heaps with girders protruding from them. This is the enemy fortress of the brickworks of Montauban. Beyond this, still further to the right, behind the old enemy line, the ground loses its monotony and passes into lovely and romantic sweeping valleys, which our men could not see from their lines.

Well behind our English lines in this district and above the dip where Carnoy stands, the fourth of the four roads from Albert runs eastward along a ridge-top between a double row of noble trees which have not suffered very severely, except at their eastern end. Just north of this road, and a little below it on the slopes of the ridge, is the village of Maricourt. Our line turns to the south-east opposite Montauban, and curves in towards the ridge so as to run just outside Maricourt, along the border of a little wood to the east of the houses. From all the high ground to the north of it, from the enemy's second line and beyond, the place is useful to give a traveller his bearings. The line of plane-trees along the road on the ridge, and the big clumps of trees round the village, are landmarks which cannot be mistaken from any part of the field.

Little is to be seen from our line outside Maricourt

Wood, except the enemy line a little beyond it, and the trees of other woods behind it.

The line turns to the south, parallel with the wood, crosses the fourth road (which goes on towards Peronne) and goes down some difficult, rather lovely, steep chalk slopes, wooded in parts, to the ruins of Fargny Mill on the Somme River.

The Somme River is here a very beautiful expanse of clear chalk water like a long wandering shallow lake. Through this shallow lake the river runs in half a dozen channels, which are parted and thwarted in many places by marsh, reed-beds, osier plots, and tracts of swampy woodland. There is nothing quite like it in England. The river-bed is pretty generally between five and six hundred yards across.

Nearly two miles above the place where the old enemy line comes down to the bank, the river thrusts suddenly north-westward, in a very noble great horse-shoe, the bend of which comes at Fargny where our lines touched it. The enemy line touched the horse-shoe close to our own at a curious wooded bank or slope, known (from its shape on the map, which is like a cocked hat) as the Chapeau de Gendarme. Just behind our lines, at the bend, the horse-shoe sweeps round to the south. The river-bed at once broadens to about two-thirds of a mile, and the river, in four or five main channels, passes under a most beautiful sweep of steep chalk cliff, not unlike some of the chalk country near Arundel. These places marked the end of the British sector at the time of the beginning of the battle. On the south or left bank of the Somme River the ground was held by the French.

CHAPTER VIII

SUCH was our old front line at the beginning of the battle, and so the travellers of our race will strive to picture it when they see the ground under the crops of coming Julys. It was never anything but a makeshift, patched together, and held, God knows how, against greater strength. Our strongest places were the half-dozen built-up observation posts at the mines near Fricourt, Serre, and La Boisselle. For the rest, our greatest strength was but a couple of sandbags deep. There was no concrete in any part of the line, very few iron girders and not many iron " humpies " or " elephant backs " to make the roofs of dugouts. The whole line gives the traveller the impression that it was improvised (as it was) by amateurs with few tools, and few resources, as best they could, in a time of need and danger. Like the old, hurriedly built Long Walls at Athens, it sufficed, and like the old camps of Cæsar it served, till our men could take the much finer lines of the enemy. A few words may be said about those enemy lines.   They were very different lines from ours.

The defences of the enemy front line varied a little in degree, but hardly at all in kind, throughout the battle-field.   The enemy wire was always deep, thick, and securely staked with iron supports, which were either crossed like the letter X, or upright, with loops to take the wire and shaped at one end like corkscrews so as to screw into the ground.   The wire stood on these supports on a thick web, about four feet high and from thirty to forty feet across.   The wire used was generally as thick as sailor's marline stuff, or two twisted rope-yarns.   It contained, as a rule, some sixteen barbs to the foot.   The wire used in front of our lines was generally galvanized, and remained grey after months of exposure.   The enemy wire, not being galvanized, rusted to a black colour, and shows up black at a great distance.   In places this web or barrier was supple-mented with trip-wire, or wire placed just above the ground, so that the artillery observing officers might not see it and so not cause it to be destroyed.   This trip-wire was as difficult to cross as the wire of the entanglements.   In one place (near the Y Ravine at Beaumont Hamel) this trip-wire was used with thin iron spikes a yard long of the kind known as calthrops. The spikes were so placed in the ground that about one foot of spike projected.   The scheme was that our men should catch their feet in the trip-wire, fall on the spikes, and be transfixed.

In places, in front of the front line in the midst of his wire, sometimes even in front of the wire, the enemy had carefully hidden snipers and machine-gun posts. Sometimes these outside posts were connected with his front-line trench by tunnels, sometimes they were simply shell-holes, slightly altered with a spade to take the snipers and the gunners. These outside snipers had some success in the early parts of the battle. They caused losses among our men by firing in the midst of them and by shooting them in the backs after they had passed. Usually the posts were small oblong pans in the mud, in which the men lay. Sometimes they were deep narrow graves in which the men stood to fire through a funnel in the earth. Here and there, where the ground was favourable, especially when there was some little knop, hillock, or bulge of ground just outside their line, as near Gommecourt Park and close to the Sunken Road at Beaumont Hamel, he placed several such posts together. Outside Gommecourt, a slight lynchet near the enemy line was prepared for at least a dozen such posts invisible from any part of our line and not easily to be picked out by photograph, and so placed as to sweep at least a mile of No Man's Land.

When these places had been passed, and the enemy

wire, more or less cut by our shrapnel, had been crossed, our men had to attack the enemy fire trenches of the first line. These, like the other defences, varied in degree, but not in kind. They were, in the main, deep, solid trenches, dug with short bays or zigzags in the pattern of the Greek Key or badger's earth. They were seldom less than eight feet and sometimes as much as twelve feet deep. Their sides were revetted, or held from collapsing, by strong wickerwork. They had good, comfortable standing slabs or banquettes on which the men could stand to fire. As a rule, the parapets were not built up with sandbags as ours were.

In some parts of the line, the front trenches were strengthened at intervals of about fifty yards by tiny forts or fortlets made of concrete and so built into the parapet that they could not be seen from without, even five yards away. These fortlets were pierced with a foot-long slip for the muzzle of a machine gun, and were just big enough to hold the gun and one gunner.

In the forward wall of the trenches were the openings of the shafts which led to the front-line dugouts. The shafts are all of the same pattern. They have open mouths about four feet high, and slant down into the earth for about twenty feet at an angle of forty-five degrees. At the bottom of the stairs which led down are the living rooms and barracks which communicate with each other so that if a shaft collapse the men below may still escape by another. The shafts and living rooms are strongly propped and panelled with wood, and this has led to the destruction of most of the few which survived our bombardment. While they were needed as billets our men lived in them. Then the wood was removed, and the dugout and shaft collapsed.

During the bombardment before an attack, the enemy kept below in his dugouts. If one shaft were blown in by a shell, they passed to the next. When the fire "lifted" to let the attack begin, they raced up the stairs with their machine guns and had them in action within a minute. Sometimes the fire was too heavy for this, for trench, parapet, shafts, dugouts, wood, and fortlets, were pounded out of existence, so that no man could say that a line had ever run there; and in these cases the garrison was destroyed in the shelters. This happened in several places, though all the enemy dugouts were kept equipped with pioneer tools by which buried men could dig themselves out.

The direction of the front-line trenches was so inclined with bends, juts, and angles as to give flanking fire upon attackers.

At some little distance behind the front line (a hundred yards or so) was a second fire line, wired like the first, though less elaborate and generally without concrete fortlets. This second line was usually as well sited for fire as the front line. There were many communication trenches between the two lines. Half a mile behind the second line was a third support line; and behind this, running along the whole front, a mile or more away, was the prepared second main position, which was in every way like the front line, with wire, concrete fortlets, dugouts, and a difficult glacis for the attacker to climb.

The enemy batteries were generally placed behind banks or lynchets which gave good natural cover; but in many places he mounted guns in strong permanent emplacements, built up of timber balks, within a couple of miles (at Fricourt within a quarter of a mile) of his front line. In woods from the high trees of which he could have clear observation, as in the Bazentin, Bernafay, and Trones Woods, he had several of these emplacements, and also stout concrete fortlets for heavy single guns.

All the enemy position on the battlefield was well gunned at the time of the beginning of the battle. In modern war, it is not possible to hide preparations for an attack on a wide front. Men have to be brought up, trenches have to be dug, the artillery has to prepare, and men, guns, and trenches have to be supplied with food, water, shells, sandbags, props, and revetments. When the fire on any sector increases tenfold, while the roads behind the lines are thronged with five times the normal traffic of troops and lorries, and new trenches, the attack or "jumping-off" trenches, are being dug in front of the line, a commander cannot fail to know that an attack is preparing. These preparations must be made and cannot be concealed from observers in the air or on the ground. The enemy knew very well that we were about to attack upon the Somme front, but did not know at which point to expect the main thrust. To be ready, in any case, he concentrated guns along the sector. It seems likely that he expected our attack to be an attempt to turn Bapaume by a thrust from the west, by Gommecourt, Puisieux, Grandcourt. In all this difficult sector his observations and arrangements for cross-fire were excellent. He concentrated a great artillery here (it is a legend among our men that he brought up a hundred batteries to defend Gommecourt alone). In this sector, and in one other place a little to the south of it, his barrage upon our trenches, before the battle, was very accurate, terrible, and deadly.

Our attacks were met by a profuse machine-gun fire from the trench parapets and from the hidden pits between and outside the lines. There was not very much rifle fire in any part of the battle, but all the hotly-fought-for strongholds were defended by machine guns to the last. It was reported that the bodies of some enemy soldiers were found chained to their guns, and that on the bodies of others were intoxicating pills, designed to madden and infuriate the takers before an attack. The fighting in the trenches was mainly done by bombing with hand-grenades, of which the enemy had several patterns, all effective. His most used type was a grey tin cylinder, holding about a pound of explosive, and screwed to a wooden baton or handle about a foot long for the greater convenience of throwing.

CHAPTER IX

EARLY in the spring of 1916, it was determined that an attack should be made by our armies upon these lines of the enemy, so as to bring about a removal of the enemy guns and men, then attacking the French at Verdun and the Russians on the eastern front.

Preparations for this attack were made throughout the first half of the year. New roads were cut, old roads were remetalled, new lines of railways were surveyed and laid, and supplies and munitions were accumulated not far from the front. Pumping stations were built and wells were sunk for the supply of water to the troops during the battle. Fresh divisions were brought up and held ready behind the line. An effort was made to check the enemy's use of aeroplanes. In June, our Air Service in the Somme sector made it so difficult for the enemy to take photographs over our lines that his knowledge of our doings along the front of the planned battle was lessened and thwarted. At the same time, many raids were made by our aeroplanes

156

upon the enemy's depots and magazines behind his front. Throughout June, our infantry raided the enemy line in many places to the north of the planned battle. It seems possible that these raids led him to think that our coming attack would be made wholly to the north of the Ancre River.

During the latter half of June, our armies concentrated a very great number of guns behind the front of the battle. The guns were of every kind, from the field gun to the heaviest howitzer. Together they made what was at that time by far the most terrible concentration of artillery ever known upon a battlefield. Vast stores of shells of every known kind were made ready, and hourly increased.

As the guns came into battery, they opened intermittent fire, so that, by the 20th of June, the fire along our front was heavier than it had been before. At the same time, the fire of the machine guns and trench mortars in our trenches became hotter and more constant. On the 24th of June this fire was increased, by system, along the front designed for the battle, and along the French front to the south of the Somme, until it reached the intensity of a fire of preparation. Knowing, as they did, that an attack was to come, the enemy made ready and kept on the alert. Throughout the front, they expected the attack for the next morning.

The fire was maintained throughout the night, but no attack was made in the morning, except by aeroplanes. These raided the enemy observation balloons, destroyed nine of them, and made it impossible for the others to keep in the air. The shelling continued all that day, searching the line and particular spots with intense fire and much asphyxiating gas. Again the enemy prepared for an attack in the morning, and again there was no attack, although the fire of preparation still went on. The enemy said, " To-morrow will make three whole days of preparation; the English will attack to-morrow." But when the morning came, there was no attack, only the never-ceasing shelling, which seemed to increase as time passed. It was now difficult and dangerous to move within the enemy lines. Relieving exhausted soldiers, carrying out the wounded, and bringing up food and water to the front, became terrible feats of war. The fire continued and increased, all that day and all the next day, and the day after that. It darkened the days with smoke and lit the nights with flashes. It covered the summer landscape with a kind of haze of hell, earth-coloured above fields and reddish above villages, from the dust of blown mud and brick flung up into the air. The tumult of these days and nights cannot be described nor imagined. The air was without wind, yet it seemed in a hurry with the passing of death. Men knew not which they heard, a roaring that was behind and in front, like a presence, or a screaming that never ceased to shriek in the air. No thunder was ever so terrible as that tumult. It broke the drums of the ears when it came singly, but when it rose up along the front and gave tongue together in full cry it humbled the soul. With the roaring, crashing, and shrieking came a racket of hammers from the machine guns till men were dizzy and sick from the noise, which thrust between skull and brain, and beat out thought. With the noise came also a terror and an exultation, that one should hurry, and hurry, and hurry, like the shrieking shells, into the pits of fire opening on the hills. Every night in all this week the enemy said, " The English will attack to-morrow," and in the front lines prayed that the attack might come, that so an end, any end, might come to the shelling.

It was fine, cloudless, summer weather, not very clear, for there was a good deal of heat haze and of mist in the nights and early mornings. It was hot, yet brisk, during the days. The roads were thick in dust. Clouds and streamers of chalk dust floated and rolled over all the roads leading to the front, till men and beasts were grey with it.

At half-past six in the morning of the 1st of July all the guns on our front quickened their fire to a pitch of intensity never before attained. Intermittent darkness.

and flashing so played on the enemy line from Gommecourt to Maricourt that it looked like a reef on a loppy
day. For one instant it could be seen as a white rim
above the wire, then some comber of a big shell struck
it fair and spouted it black aloft. Then another and
another fell, and others of a new kind came and made
a different darkness, through which now and then some
fat white wreathing devil of explosion came out and
danced. Then it would show out, with gaps in it,
and with some of it level with the field, till another
comber would fall and go up like a breaker and smash it
out of sight again. Over all the villages on the field there
floated a kind of bloody dust from the blasted bricks.

In our trenches after seven o'clock on that morning,
our men waited under a heavy fire for the signal to
attack. Just before half-past seven, the mines at half
a dozen points went up with a roar that shook the
earth and brought down the parapets in our lines.
Before the blackness of their burst had thinned or
fallen the hand of Time rested on the half-hour mark,
and along all that old front line of the English there
came a whistling and a crying. The men of the
first wave climbed up the parapets, in tumult, darkness,
and the presence of death, and having done with all
pleasant things, advanced across the No Man's Land
to begin the Battle of the Somme.